Brand and Talent

Brand and Talent

Kevin Keohane

KoganPage

LONDON   PHILADELPHIA   NEW DELHI

Reprinted 2014

First published in Great Britain and the United States in 2014 by Kogan Page Limited

2nd Floor, 45 Gee Street	1518 Walnut Street, Suite 1100	4737/23 Ansari Road
London EC1V 3RS	Philadelphia PA 19102	Daryaganj
United Kingdom	USA	New Delhi 110002
www.koganpage.com		India

© Kevin Keohane, 2014

The right of Kevin Keohane to be identified as the author of this work has been asserted by him in accordance with the Copyright, Designs and Patents Act 1988.

ISBN   978 0 7494 6925 2
E-ISBN   978 0 7494 6926 9

British Library Cataloguing-in-Publication Data

A CIP record for this book is available from the British Library.

CIP data is available
Library of Congress Control Number: 2013044128

Typeset by Graphicraft Limited, Hong Kong
Print production managed by Jellyfish
Printed and bound in Great Britain by CPI Group (UK) Ltd, Croydon CR0 4YY

*This book is dedicated to the clients I have had
the privilege of working with. Without our risks, successes
and failures together in the real world of work
(not the conference-speaking circuit), these pages would be
empty – or worse, based on someone else's theories about
reheated 'best practice' pulled off a dusty shelf. Thank you all
for believing in the power of the blank sheet of paper.*

CONTENTS

About the author   xi
Foreword   xiii
Preface   xv
Acknowledgements   xviii

01   Introduction   1

Brand and talent   1
How this book is structured   3
It isn't complicated, it's just hard   4

PART ONE   Brand   5

02   What is a brand?   7

Setting the context   7
A brief history of branding   7
Examples of great brands   10
Brand, marketing and sales   13
The value of your brand   14
Brand is a business management discipline   16
Brand and premium   17
Brand positioning   18
Conclusion   19

03   Defining your brand   20

Current state of practice   20
The challenge   26
Challenges with the current state   27
What's the problem?   29

04   Brand delivery   33

What's the point?   33
How?   34

How do you go about delivering your brand?   34
Guidelines   35
Customer and user experience   36
User experience mapping   37
Customer brand engagement   40
Employee brand engagement   41

05   Brand and social media   43

Social media is social communication... technologically
    enabled   45
Social media as an internal tool   45
Social media as an external brand engagement tool   49
Summary   50

PART TWO   Talent   51

06   The talent agenda   53

Before, during and after people join you   53
A bit of the history   54
CLC engagement model   55
CLC's HR EVP framework   56
Why do organizations struggle, then?   57
Functional ownership of the brand and talent agenda   58

07   Engaging talent   63

It is a journey   63
The employee lifecycle   64
The building blocks of employee communications   75
Before we get started...   75
Diversity   77
Messages   79
Media   83
Measurement   83
Summary   86
Are you ready?   86

PART THREE   Brand and talent   89

08   A better way   91

Making the connection   91
Where to begin?   92
How is this different from other approaches?   102

09   Purpose   104

A star to steer by   104
Getting to a Purpose   105
Is your Purpose your slogan or tagline?   106
Is this a brand model then?   106
What is a Purpose-driven brand?   106
What evidence is there that Purpose-driven brands do
    any better than others?   109
Summary   111

10   Ambition   113

Summary   116

11   Strategy   117

What is the plan?   117
Examples   118
Summary   121

12   Proposition   123

What is the deal?   123
Positioning   123
Proposition   127

13   Putting it all together   129

Putting P-A-S-P to work   129
Friction points   130
Is employer branding the right approach any more?   131
One brand   131

The integrated approach   133
Network analysis   134
It applies to every function   137
Testing the approach   139
Summary   139

14   **Toolkit**   141

Exercise one: Value disciplines   141
Exercise two: Positioning   144
Exercise three: Purpose, Ambition, Strategy, Positioning   145
Exercise four: Stakeholders   145
Exercise five: Messaging framework   152
Exercise six: Bringing it all together   153

PART FOUR   Insight interviews   155

15   **Brand and executive talent – Bob Benson**   157

16   **Brand and diversity – Beth Brooke**   161

17   **Brand, talent and the new world of work – Dave Coplin**   168

18   **Brand, talent and strategy – Mike Cullen**   175

19   **Brand in a multinational conglomerate – S P Shukla**   183

20   **Brand and purpose – Michael Sneed**   190

21   **Brand and talent – Mark Weinberger**   197

Glossary   202
Talent management terms   204
Resources and suggested reading   208
Index   215

ABOUT THE AUTHOR

Kevin Keohane is uniquely positioned to provide advice on the intersection of brand management and talent management – his career has seen him live and work the world over in roles spanning marketing, public relations, branding, change management, employee communications and human resources consulting.

Living and working from North America to Australasia to Scandinavia and Europe ignited an interest in cross-cultural communication and globalization. Passionate about brand, talent and organizational development as a complex, adaptive system, if he has a Purpose it is to abolish the mile-deep, inch-wide functional mindsets within organizations that hinder their ability to deliver against their loftier ambitions.

Currently a Partner at BrandPie in London/New York, he most recently led the agency team supporting Ernst & Young's (now EY) global repositioning efforts. He works closely with CEOs and boards of multinationals to help them clarify and express their brands more effectively in their global and local marketplaces. Previously he named, built and led the global 'Brand and Talent' practice for the Publicis Groupe.

He has also worked in the world of employee engagement and employer branding, having led efforts to express employment value propositions for BP, The Coca-Cola Company Europe ('What's your secret formula?'), Coca-Cola Greater China and Coca-Cola Enterprises ('THIRST'). He helped EY develop its highly successful 'whole of life' employment value proposition – 'No matter when you join or however long you stay, the exceptional EY experience will last a lifetime.' His other employer branding and employee engagement experience spans a range of organizations from Allen & Overy, American Express and Barclays to BP, Capgemini, Carphone Warehouse, EY, The Gates Corporation, Kellogg's, Mars, Nokia, Orange, KPMG, Vodafone and many others.

He is a regular conference speaker and has written extensively in the trade press on brand, talent and employee engagement. He was selected to write the chapter 'Advanced employee engagement' for the latest edition of the *Gower Handbook of Employee Communications* and is author of the popular book, *The Talent Journey: The 55-minute guide to employee communications*. He co-founded the Intranet Benchmarking Forum (IBF) having developed its core methodologies, and established the UK User Experience Professionals' Association (as its first President).

A graduate of the University of Denver and of the Georgetown University Institute on Political Journalism, Kevin is also a Fellow of the Institute of Internal Communications (IoIC) and an Accredited Business Communicator (ABC), awarded by the IABC. He has won numerous awards for his work (if only he remembered where they all were).

When not doing brand and talent stuff, he is a musician, avid motorcyclist and fitness fanatic. He makes his home in London with his wife Nicky and their Bombay cat, Barbarella.

Contact him on LinkedIn anytime.

FOREWORD

Many business leaders forget the power of brand management and talent management as two key drivers of innovation and business growth. Some do understand the impact that each can have, independently. But as this book points out, leading organizations are discovering that brand and talent can operate in concert together to drive even greater business impact.

I have always believed that brand and talent are two sides of the same coin. Smart organizations, particularly in the service industry, realize that their people are their brand in the marketplace. This book clearly sets out that the best growth agenda is a talent agenda.

At EY, we understand the benefits of connecting brand, employer brand, human resources and employee engagement – something clearly demonstrated in this book. In 2011, I set about proving to the business that there is a direct correlation between not only the engagement of our people and how our brand is perceived in the marketplace, but also between the engagement of our people and retention levels and revenue per person. In what became known as the 'Business Linkage Survey', we demonstrated that increased engagement positively affects brand image. We did this by comparing the engagement index from our people survey and the favourability index from our brand survey. We clearly showed that increased engagement affects the cost of recruitment – with a sizeable variation in retention rates between the most- and least-engaged business units. We also revealed the link between engagement and revenue per person, to the tune of a difference of tens of thousands of dollars in revenue per person between our most engaged and least engaged business units.

We had the businesses' attention.

It's widely accepted in EY now that the engagement of our people – before, during and even after their employment with us – helps set us apart as an organization, increasing our competitive advantage in a complex, diversifying and globalizing business world.

Our employment value proposition has since become 'whenever you join, however long you stay, the exceptional experience you get at EY will last you a lifetime'. This applies not just to the 175,000 people who work at

EY currently, but the 1 million or so 'brand ambassadors' (those who have worked here) out in the marketplace.

A talent agenda based on this scale, directly linked to the brand, is virtually limitless in its potential in terms of business growth.

Our business purpose, *Building a better working world*, perfectly articulates the reason why we exist. It's an idea that was generated from the inside out, validated with our clients and stakeholders the world over, and it serves to ensure we never lose sight of the higher sense of purpose that drives us as individuals and as an organization. Building a better working world is what we do: for our clients, our people and the communities in which we live and work.

It's helped clarify the link between what we say and what we do every day. We now not only think about brand and talent in a completely different way, but we also apply this new way of thinking to the way we manage our whole organization.

In short, we have set about connecting our talent proposition and our brand proposition. This more integrated approach resonates well both inside and outside the organization, something I hope our example, and this book, will help other organizations achieve.

Mike Cullen, Global People Leader, EY

PREFACE

When Henry Ford set out to give people the Model T in any colour they wanted as long as it was black, he designed the organization he needed in order to bring the Model T to them. He knew that the most efficient way to build a car, given the technology and workforce he had at his disposal, was to break the task into steps.

He created the assembly line: each worker had a specific task related to one specific component of the automobile's construction in an efficient sequence. Workers could be trained to do one thing, to do it well, to do it with minimal supervision, and to do it fast. They were motivated and rewarded accordingly.

The 'scientific management' thinking that likely led Ford to this approach had been pioneered by Frederick Winslow Taylor. Taylor is held to be one of the grandfathers of management consulting as we know it today, and he held clear – and very influential – views on the efficient management of business:

> It is only through enforced standardization of methods, enforced adoption of the best implements and working conditions, and enforced cooperation that this faster work can be assured. And the duty of enforcing the adoption of standards and enforcing this cooperation rests with management alone.[1]

There has been startlingly little change in the way we organize our enterprises today. Modern management consulting techniques involving analysis and process improvement is a multi-hundred-billion-dollar industry.

The thing is, adhering to these old management models is fast becoming more risky than taking the steps to change them for the better. Dan Pink makes this observation in his book *Drive*. Taylor's style of motivation and management can be effective for repetitive, or as Pink calls them, 'algorithmic', types of task:

> An algorithmic task is one in which you follow a set of established instructions down a single pathway to one conclusion.[2]

But Pink points out that numerous studies of motivation demonstrate clearly and unequivocally that when it comes to more creative or 'problem solving' (heuristic) tasks, this approach is not only ineffective but counter-productive.

In short: people perform worse when managed and motivated in this carrot-and-stick manner.

Ford was facing challenges of a very similar nature to chief executives today: a shortage of skilled talent; limited employee communication and collaboration; a need to grow while maximizing margin; a complex and expensive supply chain.[3]

The organization of the modern enterprise has remained largely unchanged for more than 50 years. So what has changed since the Model Ts began rolling off the production line in October 1908? Short answer: the emergence of talent, information and communication into isolated structures, the hallmark of which is the organizational silo.

In my 25 years of working across the related functional disciplines of brand, marketing, PR, human resources, and internal communication, the single prevailing theme – and the prevailing source of failure, duplication, waste, inefficiency and squandered opportunity – has been the organizational silo.

The specialist begets this silo. And that is where the trouble begins. I'm not for a minute saying we don't need specialists. They are critical.

Developing a specialist skill set and a set of competencies for a modern marketplace became sensible and valuable. We have moved from the age of the specialist into an age where specialist skills alone are necessary, but not sufficient, to drive growth in the modern organization. I like to refer to this as the 'T' – where 'specialists' with mile-deep, inch-wide expertise are the downstroke, while 'generalists' with inch-deep, mile-wide expertise are the cross-stroke.

So, this is not a book about radical organizational design innovation. Instead, it is a book that looks at integrating some closely related disciplines that lie at the heart of the successful business of the future. These related disciplines provide one of the clearest opportunities to integrate old-world specialist silos into a more effective whole.

This is not a book about branding. It is not a book about human resources, employee engagement or talent management.

It is a book about the *integration* of brand and talent management at the strategic decision-making level, so that it permeates every facet of an organization's operations. And it's about how this integration can serve as a powerful way to enhance effectiveness and efficiency in building and defending your reputation as an organization, inside and out, so that you are more profitable and productive in executing a strategy that helps you to achieve your ambition and fulfil your purpose.

Notes

1   Taylor, F W (1911) *The Principles of Scientific Management*, Harper & Brothers, New York

2   Pink, D (2011) *Drive: The surprising truth about what motivates us*, Canongate Books, New York

3   Case, G *et al* (2007) *Service Management Strategies That Work: Guidance for executives*, Van Haren Publishing, Amersfoort, The Netherlands

ACKNOWLEDGEMENTS

Thanks, in no particular order, to a wide range of people who have made writing this possible:

My wife, Nicky, for putting up with many weekends, days and evenings spent in my studio when I should have been doing something with her (and our cat, Bella).

Dave Allen and Roger Partington at BrandPie for their unwavering belief and support.

Dan Gray, my partner in crime on too many of these occasions.

Jeremy Sice for 'getting it' when so many others didn't.

The CommScrum movement, and its co-founders (Dan, Lindsay and Mike), for not letting niceties get in the way of a good ruck.

Lanny, Daylon, Laura, Wendie and the team at Capgemini who were fun and challenging on the clock (and off it).

Barbara Davies and several hundred other people at EY who kept us on our toes but kept the faith throughout.

My trusty researcher, Hannah Stuart-Leach, who could turn random questions and musings into 10-page research reports seemingly effortlessly.

The executives who generously gave their time to talk about the ideas in this book: Bob Benson, Beth Brooke, Mike Cullen, Dave Coplin, S P Shukla, Michael Sneed, Mark Weinberger and Richard Burton (whose transcript was alas eaten by the proverbial dog).

Introduction

Brand and talent

Your brand management and talent management approaches are two of the most powerful levers at your disposal in driving tangible, measurable improvement to the performance of your business.

Brand management helps ensure that people are aware of you, of what you can do for them and why they should consider and purchase from you. It gives you something clear to stand for and to steer by; it guides some of your biggest strategic decisions. Name something more important to a CEO than the reputation of his or her firm.

Talent management helps you make sure you get the right people aboard to help in the first place, and then create an environment where they can contribute more so that your organization can deliver on its promises. Name something more important to a CEO than the talent needed to deliver growth.

Chances are, they are both in the top five; for some, the top three, according to recent surveys by McKinsey, PWC and BCG. But the two are inextricably linked – a fact that seems to be lost on many boards, CEOs and strategists today.

Why do so many organizations manage these distinct drivers of business effectiveness as if they are completely different things? This book seeks to answer that question, and it makes the case for a different (integrated) approach to thinking about the way your organization manages the way it attracts, recruits, develops and motivates the people it needs to thrive, in order to provide a product or service that is authentic, relevant to its customers and differentiated from its competitors – for both business and talent. Does that sound crazy?

It still does to some people. When I set out to create the idea of 'Brand and Talent' as a practice area in one of the world's biggest global communication networks five years ago, I encountered surprising resistance to the very name

'Brand and Talent' itself. They just didn't get it. *Brand?* That's about external positioning. Logos. PR and advertising campaigns. Reputation management. Social media. *Talent?* That's about recruiting. Employee communications. Human resources. 'They just don't go together. It'll confuse the marketplace.'

One of the most telling challenges in writing a book that sets out to make the case for integrating several related disciplines is how easy or hard it is to research those disciplines. *Brand?* There is a lot out there about how to define, create, activate, maintain, defend and grow your brand in the marketplace. *Talent?* There is even more out there about talent acquisition, talent management, employee engagement, motivation and the many human resources techniques to help make the most of talent.

But *Brand and Talent?* While, to be fair, the world of 'employer branding' has grown in profile, as has the idea of 'living the brand', these are still generally seen to be separate activities aimed at solving different challenges. While there is evidence of some organizations and service providers connecting employer branding and living the brand/employee brand engagement-type activities, they are far from being integrated and hardwired to the organization – at either communication, operational process or management level. It is virtually impossible to find an actual example of where brand, employer brand, human resources and employee engagement have been genuinely connected and managed as a single integrated process.

But the tide is turning. The now irrational (yet at one time perfectly sensible) functional separation of many of the activities relating to brand management and talent management has reached the end of its usefulness. Smart organizations understand that there is a better way – that one core idea is better than many when it comes to focus and clarity in a dynamic internal and external environment.

Importantly, the first six chapters of this book cover some fairly traditional approaches to brand management and talent engagement. For most experts, these chapters will probably not tell you much that you don't already know. It may even feel a bit patronizing. For those readers who are experts, feel free to jump straight to Chapter 8, where the approach we developed at BrandPie is explored and explained. It's a powerful model, and one that we have successfully used with organizations facing significant repositioning opportunities such as EY (formerly Ernst & Young), Capgemini Applications in North America, and others.

How this book is structured

Be aware: this book has many short chapters. This is deliberate. I expect that most of my readers are busy business people who probably won't read this book in a small number of sittings, probably won't read the whole thing from cover to cover, and prefer to get their information in bite-size chunks between meetings, cab rides and plane journeys. The philosophy is similar to the approach taken in my book *The Talent Journey: The 55-minute guide to employee communications*. You'll find some of that thinking represented here. I like short, sharp, and to the point.

Perhaps ironically, the best way to approach this topic is to break up the pieces and address them separately before bringing them together. (Taylor would be proud!) Only then can the case be made for a more integrated approach to managing brand and talent.

So this book will first take you through the principles and theory of *brand*. While there are many books on brand, we will cover a very pragmatic approach to defining, building and deploying your brand. This is not going to be the approach to branding that dominated the previous generation (a world of brand models, brand values, brand attributes, brand essences) – although it will touch on these. They have their place, but all too often serve to exacerbate efficiency-sapping functional divisions between brand and talent management.

Then, we will go through the principles of *talent*. We'll run from talent acquisition and recruiting through to a very high-level look at talent management and a discussion on employee engagement and its links to brand and business performance. This won't be a deep dive into the minutia of performance management and competency frameworks, although it will touch on these and other issues. Again, the case will be made that often the focus on the 'means justifying the end' process-focused approach only deepens functional divides and diminishes your organization's effectiveness.

Third, we will connect the two and explore how *brand* and *talent* are two sides of the same coin. You'll get a selection of templates, tools and techniques to manage this process for your consideration, adaptation, modification and use. These are many of the tools I actually use in real life with clients. Used effectively, they can make a big difference in getting people aligned to the 'Brand and Talent' way of thinking.

Fourth, and in my opinion most importantly, there are interviews with some of the world's leading thinkers in this area – each looking at the challenge from different perspectives: the CEO, the CMO, Corporate Affairs head, the People lead, the Executive Recruiter, and so on. Real-life points of view validate the points made in this book.

It isn't complicated, it's just hard

It's a cliché to say that the soft stuff is the hard stuff. The real challenge lies not in functional expertise in brand management, nor in the disciplines of employee engagement and human resource and talent management. It is in having clarity of purpose, focus, discipline and willpower to take the steps necessary to align these functional activities in a more consolidated and coherent manner. And this means upsetting the traditional functional apple cart. If you don't have the stomach for it, you might want to stop reading now.

Having been involved in literally dozens of projects with a range of organizations the world over, across industries, cultures, geographies, management styles and economic conditions, over more than 20 years, I don't want to appear cynical. Yet one thing is certain: the reason most efforts to engage people internally and externally in your organization's purpose, ambition, strategy and brand fail to deliver is an outmoded, functionally driven way of thinking. The irresistible force of integrated, aligned senior executive thinking will meet the immovable object of functional mindsets with perspectives on what is important – and territory to defend.

The organizational silo is alive and well. It has deep roots and is often protected by long, sharp thorns. Its head is shaped to provide a view that is deeply biased towards one way of looking at – and interpreting – the world it perceives. It feels vulnerable and insecure emerging into the brightly lit (and frighteningly level) playing field that is The Big Picture.

The silo always promises to cooperate with other silos. It assures you that it is collaborating cross-functionally, that it is consulting and sharing information. It nods knowingly when you ask it if it has considered The Big Picture. Don't believe it.

Whether through gently leading it to water, or forcing it to drink through formal restructuring, this book lays out the case for taking a more integrated approach to brand and talent management that, when taken to its ultimate conclusion, can and should result in changes not only to the way you think about brand and talent, but to the way you manage your organization and its strategy. In so doing, your organization and its people should reap the benefits of a more effective, efficient, cohesive and – perhaps most importantly – vastly simplified approach to connecting your people to the service you deliver.

PART ONE
Brand

What is a brand? | 02

Setting the context

Your brand is your *reputation*. It's that simple.

What does someone think when they hear or see your name? Do they recognize it? Do they have a positive or negative reaction? Do they have a clear idea of who you are and what you stand for?

This chapter sets out a brief history of branding to help establish some context, and a review of prevailing brand development and management techniques you are likely to encounter. But more importantly, it lays the foundation for later exploring a more integrated approach to managing your brand in a way that is clear, simple, and reduces much of the complexity (and a lot of the cross-silo duplication and redundancy) that traditional branding methods generate.

A brief history of branding

Why did human beings begin the practice of branding in the first place?

To insure honesty, provide quality assurance, identify source or ownership, hold producers responsible, differentiate, as a form of identification and to create emotional bonding. Interestingly, people value brands for many of the same reasons today. Clearly, history provides some insight and perspective on modern day branding (Table 2.1).[1]

TABLE 2.1   A brief history of branding

Date	Event
1300 BC	So, how far back does branding go? At least 5,000 years. • Potters' marks were used on pottery and porcelain in China, Greece, Rome and India. • Branding of cattle and livestock go back as far as 2000 BC. • Archaeologists have found evidence of advertising among Babylonians dating back to 3000 BC.[1]
1800s 1890s	• Rise of 'Pitchmen', a mixture of sales people and a precursor to Mad Men advertisers.[2] • Towards the end of the 19th century a collection of new technology and methods of communication such as the invention of mail order catalogues, the advancement of railroads and the expansion of the postal service drives a massive shift in attitudes to products and purchasing of things.[3] • In 1876, after the United Kingdom passed the Trade Mark Registration Act, Bass Ale became the first trademarked brand in the world.
1930s	• In 1931, P&G ad man Neil McElroy sent round his now-famous memo explaining why P&G should have a brand team for each product, paving the way for modern brand management.[4]
1940s	• The concept of the Unique Selling Proposition (USP) emerges – ranging from Lucky Strikes' 'Reach for a Lucky instead of a sweet' to help weight loss to IBM's THINK campaign.[5]
1950s and 60s	• 'Brands like Tide, Kraft and Lipton set the benchmarks for consumer branding. This marked the start of almost 50 years of marketing where "winning" was determined by understanding the consumer better than your competitors and getting the total "brand mix" right. The brand mix is more than the logo, or the price of a product. It's also the packaging, the promotions, and the advertising, all of which is guided by precisely worded positioning statements.'[6] • 'By the mid-1960s we enter the 'Mad Men' Era where we see major brands becoming something more than just a product, from Harley Davison to Adidas to Mercedes, be they a believer in counter culture or harbour an idealistic status symbol, selling the myth of the culture with a brand had become fundamental.'[7]

TABLE 2.1 *Continued*

Date	Event
1980s	• Society starts questioning brands; the language used in advertising – eg Nike's business practices – was being questioned; Calvin Klein's treatment of models; and numerous others.[8]
Early 1990s	• 'Commoditization leads to a quest for authenticity: one by one the big retailers started to realize that they had an opportunity to also play the branding game and that by selling more, higher quality, but particularly better-branded products, they could not only dramatically improve their margin mix, but they could raise the profile and reputation of their own brand as a whole.'[9]
2000s	• The retail landscape in the UK pioneers retail branding – and is different to elsewhere as a result. Retailers such as Tesco, Waitrose and Sainsbury started hiring marketers from their suppliers like Unilever and P&G in the 1980s and 1990s. Today these companies and their portfolio of brands enjoy equal and sometimes better brand loyalty than any of the manufacturer brands they carry.[10] • The profit margins of these UK supermarket chains are over double that of the rest of the world's supermarkets.[11] • Unilever pioneered corporate rebranding when they unveiled the new U logo in the early 2000s, made up of interconnecting images symbolic of the brand categories they represent.[12]
2011	• The explosion of branded offerings is overwhelming and confusing consumers and causing an ever-increasing headache for the leaders of 'traditional' brands.[13] • The average Western consumer is exposed to 2,000–3,000 brand messages a day.[14]
Today	• Globalization and the advent of social media make brand recommendations many-to-many, not just one-to-many or one-to-one.[15]

Notes to Table 2.1

1 Daye, D (2006 [accessed 11 October 2013]) History of Branding, *Branding Strategy Insider* [Online] http://www.brandingstrategyinsider.com

2 Kurtuldu, M [accessed 11 October 2013] Brand New: The History of Branding, *Design Today*, www.designtoday.info

3 Kurtuldu [accessed 11 October 2013]

4 Lundgaard, J (2013 [accessed 11 October 2013]) Five lessons in corporate brand building from the big boys [Online] http://econsultancy.com/uk/blog/62742-five-lessons-in-corporate-brand-building-from-the-big-boys

5 Lundgaard (2013)

6 de Swaan Arons, M (2011 [accessed 11 October 2013]) How brands were born: a brief history of modern marketing, *The Atlantic*

7 Kurtuldu [accessed 11 October 2013]

8 Kurtuldu [accessed 11 October 2013]

9 de Swaan Arons (2011)

10 de Swaan Arons (2011)

11 de Swaan Arons (2011)

12 Lundgaard (2013)

13 de Swaan Arons (2011)

14 *The New York Times* (2007) Anywhere the eye can see, it's likely to see an ad, 15 January

15 Richardson, N (2012 [accessed 11 October 2013]) A Quick History of Branding, *The Branding Spot* [Online] http://ndrichardson.com/blog/2012/07/03/a-quick-history-of-branding/

Examples of great brands

While great brands are often household names with substantial brand-building budgets – and score high in 'sex appeal' – the real secret behind a great brand is that it does something very simple. Great brands are single-minded and clear about what they promise. Great brands then deliver on that promise.

The implication is that any organization can create a great brand, regardless of its size and its resources. In fact, the larger, more complex and global an organization is, the harder it becomes to stay true to knowing what that promise is, and ensuring its delivery.

When you look at a list of 'great brands' that have significant emotional and financial value, invariably you will see businesses that are crystal clear on delivering on their promise and unwavering in their focus on it (Table 2.2). The phrase 'ruthless consistency' applies. When these brands falter, it is almost always when they lose focus on their promise and ensuring its delivery.

You will also find that the brand is not just a logo or a function of marketing – understanding the promise and ensuring its delivery is hardwired into every management metric and process in the business, from supply chain to budgeting to talent attraction and management.

TABLE 2.2   Examples of great brands

Brand	Description
Coca-Cola	'Coke's brand promise of fun, freedom, and refreshment resonates nearly everywhere. The company excels at keeping the brand fresh while maintaining a powerful sense of nostalgia that unites generations of Coke lovers and reinforces consumers' deep connections to the brand.'[1]
Apple	The Apple brand remains the poster child for how to build a great global brand – a relentless focus on never settling for what the consumer thinks they want, and creating something they never imagined they needed. Captured in 'Think different,' Apple certainly does – and the hard work of maintaining that focus has driven their phenomenal success globally.
Amazon	Amazon has achieved their success for a variety of reasons – but their entire ecosystem is open, with one idea at its heart: 'Content is geared toward *you*. Whoever *you* are, Amazon gets you.' Amazon uses content optimization, user generated content to build credibility, and relentless use of data to generate insight about its customers.[2] 'With over 200 million customers worldwide, not to mention the millions of shoppers that use Amazon for research to help make the purchase decision, Amazon shopping continues to shape shopper experiences and set new standards for retail.'[3]
Virgin Atlantic	Virgin Atlantic built a brand by redefining their category – they looked at the entire experience of flying, not just the time spent aboard the aircraft. According to Richard Branson, 'A brand name that is known internationally for innovation, quality and a sense of fun is what we have always aspired to with Virgin.' The role of the airline itself has been that of matching the reality of the product with the values created by the image.[4]

TABLE 2.2   *Continued*

Brand	Description
WL Gore Associates	Ranked 10 on *The Sunday Times 2013 Best Companies to Work For* list: 'WL GORE & ASSOCIATES (UK) is best known for its Gore-Tex fabrics. Since its inception in 1958, the company has worked to develop innovative electronics, fabrics and industrial and medical products. But innovation at the creative technologies firm does not stop at the production line. It is notable among its employees for an idiosyncratic structural quirk – it defines itself as a workplace without managers.'[5]
Goldman Sachs	The inclusion of an investment bank given the current economy might raise eyebrows, but Goldman Sachs is a household name synonymous with high-performance investing. Given the relentless negativity and perhaps even the perception of arrogance, Goldman Sachs continues to maintain significant brand equity and leadership in its industry. They continue to attract clients' capital. They continue to promise to grow your investment.
Accenture	It's hard to avoid the Accenture brand if you travel anywhere in the world. Their ruthless consistency to a single idea – 'High performance. Delivered.' – never, ever varies. Look at their website, ask their clients, ask their people, everything they say and do follows that guiding idea.
HSBC	Again ubiquitous for the business traveller, HSBC sets the standard for owning the 'Global – Local' message through ruthless focus on the core idea of 'The world's local bank.' Their campaigns flex and variations on this theme continue, but HSBC never diverges from the core idea. Like Accenture, this is carried through to their talent attraction efforts as well.

1 Interbrand, *Best Global Brands* (BrandZ), 2012

2 Richardson, B (2012 [accessed 11 October 2013]) A Brand Case Study: Amazon, *Content Equals Money* [Online] http://contentequalsmoney.com/a-brand-case-study-amazon/

3 Zybowski, A (2013) *BrandZ™ Top 100 Most Valuable Global Brands*, Interbrand, 2013

4 The Times 100 Business Case Studies [Online] http://businesscasestudies.co.uk/virgin-atlantic/building-an-airline-through-brand-values/the-branson-factor.html#ixzz2UgmTnzpJ [accessed 11 October 2013]

5 *The Sunday Times, Best 100 Companies To Work For*, 2013

Defining what a brand is – your reputation – is easy. How you influence your reputation – the approaches you take to defining, managing, growing, defending, raising the awareness and value of your reputation – is more challenging.

Brand, marketing and sales

Never forget that brand management can be a powerful business building tool in its own right – when properly managed, your brand can become more than a marketing tool and should drive, strengthen, align and accelerate your strategy. And, of course, the role of brand management is to play a central role in positively influencing marketplace perception – in terms of the talent market, the commercial market, and the marketplace occupied by other stakeholders who have influence on, or are influenced by, your organization and its activities.

Your marketing and communication efforts have, as discussed earlier, much more limited impact than you might imagine. A good rule of thumb is that 70–75 per cent of your reputation is dictated by what you do, the performance of the products and services you provide, the environments in which you provide them and the behaviour of your people. The remaining 25–35 per cent of perception is created through your brand, marketing and communication efforts.

A fundamental model is the 'marketing funnel' (Figure 2.1). It demonstrates the need to influence audiences to move deeper into a continuum ranging from awareness to advocacy. Clearly, people need to be Aware of you as a business to consider any engagement. Then, they need to include you in

FIGURE 2.1   The brand marketing funnel

their Consideration set among other alternatives. Through trial and adoption they will develop Preference and, ideally, become Advocates.

Creating Awareness, in and of itself, is not sufficient to drive brand value. It's a start. But your efforts must be coordinated and effective in order to move people along the funnel to the points of Preference (for our purposes, we'll consider this conversion into a sale) and Advocacy (where customers become ambassadors for your brand).

This is illustrated in the model shown in Figure 2.2, based on a real case study where the number one player was losing market share to a challenger despite greater Awareness in the marketplace and comparable positions. You can blanket the market with advertising and communications, but if you have failed to create a bond – engagement – with talent, customers or stakeholders, it will prove difficult and costly to convert them into Advocates.

FIGURE 2.2   Efficient vs inefficient conversion

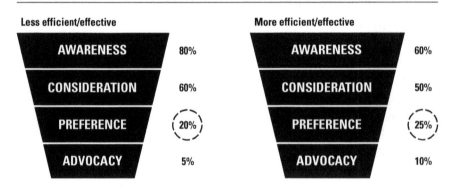

The story is true for talent, customers and other stakeholders in terms of their willingness to support your business and brand, to be neutral or ignore it, or, in the worst case, actively resist it and become a so-called 'brand assassin'. In the world of increasing access to information and social media, and where statistics show that negative brand experiences are often more publicized than positive ones, it's an important principle to consider.

The value of your brand

If this business were split up, I would give you the land and bricks and mortar, and I would take the brands and trade marks, and I would fare better than you.
(John Stuart, Chairman of Quaker, ca. 1900)

Your brand has significant financial value – depending on your industry, anywhere from 10 per cent to upwards of 50 per cent or more. The London Stock Exchange endorsed the concept of brand valuation in 1989 by allowing the inclusion of intangible assets when seeking shareholder approval in acquisitions:

> Brands will be major drivers of corporate value in the 21st century. Investors and business leaders have recognized this. Financial managers and planners are increasingly using brand equity tracking models to facilitate business planning.[2]

There are many approaches to brand valuation:

Assessing attributes (Aker and others)[3]

This means assessment of attributes such as satisfaction, loyalty, awareness, market share either tracked separately or weighted according to industry. Young & Rubicam has also developed a 'Brand Asset Valuator' – an attribute assessment approach based on Differentiation, Relevance, Esteem and Knowledge. Others no doubt exist but the concept remains the same. Such methods often use an assigned value, rather than a measured value, and thus are subject to challenge.

Brand equity (Moran)[4]

This approach combines three elements – *Effective Market Share* (the sum of market shares in all segments, weighted by each segment's proportion of total sales); *Relative Price*, a ratio of the price of goods sold under a given brand, divided by the average price of comparable goods in the market; and *Durability*, the percentage of customers who will buy that brand in the following year.

Brand valuation[5]

Brand valuation methods seek to take the most robust financial data available to the model in order to arrive at a plausible valuation of a brand. While these methods are also subject to challenge, they at least strive to create as objective as possible a view of a brand's strength.

Interbrand[6] performs an annual valuation published as 'The BrandZ Top 100 Most Valuable Brands' report. This uses a company's financial data as well as market dynamics and an assessment of the role of a brand in income generation, and then forecasts the future on the basis of brand strength and risk.

Brand Finance[7] publishes its own Global 500 study annually using a 'royalty relief' approach that calculates the net present value of the hypothetical royalty payments an organization would receive if it licensed its brand to a third party.

An increasingly popular measure is 'net promoter score' or NPS. NPS is a metric developed by Fred Reichheld, Bain & Company, and Satmetrix.[8] Its power is its simplicity. Customers are asked *'How likely are you to recommend company/brand/product X to a friend/colleague/relative?'* and score their response from 0 to 10. Promoters give a 9 or 10 score, Passives a 7 or 8, and Detractors a 0 to 6 score. The NPS score is the percentage of *Promoters* less the percentage of *Detractors* and ranges from –100 to +100.

All of these methods have strengths and weaknesses, but the important thing is to establish that an organization's brand is an intangible asset that is worth a significant amount of money – and it should be respected and managed accordingly.

Brand is a business management discipline

Do you place enough emphasis on managing your reputation as a discipline of strategic management, rather than a responsibility of the marketing function? Dave Allen[9] lays out some questions that should lead you to a long, hard look at how you manage your brand as a strategic asset:

- Does the brand name of your company open doors?
- Is it easy to get meetings?
- Do potential business partners bring you ideas to invest in?
- Do you attract the best talent?
- Do good people stay more than 2–3 years?
- Are your people driven to get the job done?
- Do your customers advocate you, or simply tolerate you? Are they willing to forgive you when you make a mistake?
- Has your share price increased steadily in value over time?
- Do you make margin that allows you to invest and grow and is the envy of your competition?

By asking these questions, you can very quickly establish not only whether you believe you have a strong reputation, but also some very basic parameters around where some of your challenges and opportunities might lie.

The answers to these questions, often uncomfortable, serve as a powerful starting point to move forward your organization's conversations about building, managing and defending your reputation in your marketplace.

Brand and premium

The final idea in this chapter is that all of this should lead you to an interesting and sometimes unexpected conclusion: your reputation determines in many ways your ability to command a premium for your products and services.

In their book *The Discipline of Market Leaders*,[10] Treacy and Wiersema ask a similar question: why do some companies outperform others, often within a virtually homogeneous category?

Through a study of market leaders across sectors and industries, such as Wal-Mart, Dell, Southwest Airlines, Cott, Airborne Express, Atlantic Richfield, Home Depot, Intel and Sony a very clear theme emerged. And while their book is about strategic management (I don't think the word brand appears at all), the implications for reputation management are clear.

According to Treacy and Wiersema, there are three areas in which an organization can achieve market leadership:

- *Product or service leadership*. You charge a premium because you produce the best product or service.

- *Operational excellence*. You charge a premium because your end-to-end processes are simply more efficient in getting your product or service to market than your competitors.

- *Customer/marketplace intimacy*. Your insight into the client/ customer, their industry and their market – from solutions to relationship management to results – allows you to outperform the competition and charge more.

What's the trick? You pick *one* that you focus on. You only need to be as good as the competition at the other two.

The value discipline model is certainly open to challenge and debate, particularly in a world where disruptive technology has rendered some elements very difficult to attain leadership in (the internet was in its infancy and not really in the public domain when Treacy and Wiersema published their first article!).

But the value of the exercise is that the implications for brand and reputation management are clear: you can't try to be all things to all people.

You need to focus your business. The decisions you make on what you want to focus your business on drive what you want your reputation in the market to be.

Brand positioning

This should lead you to brand positioning – in other words, what you stand for and how you want to be perceived by all of your different stakeholders in all of the many different ways they will experience the things you say and do as an organization.

A great brand positioning must simultaneously do three things. Your positioning must be:

- *Authentic.* Your positioning must be an accurate and true reflection of your organization – what it believes in, what its culture and values are, how it really reacts in any given situation. Organizations that try to be something that they are not are generally unsuccessful – particularly in the era of social media and increased transparency and access to information by virtually all of your stakeholders regarding virtually every aspect of your organization's operation, wherever it operates.

- *Relevant.* In addition to being true, your positioning has to be relevant to the stakeholders you are seeking to influence. If what you are saying is not of interest or not aligned to the interests of those whom you seek to turn into advocates, it doesn't matter how true or different your brand is – it just won't matter to them.

- *Different.* It might be true, it might be relevant, but it has to be different... and be different in a way that matters. Differentiation is where your value discipline generates a premium price or greater margin than your competitors.

There are many models and approaches to achieving a clear and differentiating brand positioning – and we will discuss what I believe is a more integrated and powerful approach in Chapter 8. But the key is less about the techniques you employ and more about your intent: how honest, how disciplined, how united and how focused your organization is in genuinely answering the questions and challenging itself to overcome the many barriers that get in the way of a genuinely market-moving positioning.

Conclusion

What do you stand for? What do you want to be known for? Why should people buy from you, or want to come to work for you? Why would they pay more for what you do?

The answers to these questions bring to life the thesis of this book – that while a significant amount of the effort and investment in building and managing your reputation sits with the marketing function, a great deal more of it actually lives in the decisions being made in, and the operations of, virtually every other function in the business.

The next chapter deals with approaches to developing, building and managing your brand – based on the foundations we have laid down in this chapter.

Notes

1   Daye, D (2006 [accessed 11 October 2013]) History of Branding, *Branding Strategy Insider* [Online] http://www.brandingstrategyinsider.com

2   Brand Finance (2010) White Paper, Connecting Brand Value, 'Brand Equity' and Brand Economics, *Brand Finance* [Online] http://brandfinance.com/knowledge_centre/whitepapers/connecting-brand-value-brand-equity-and-brand-economics

3   Farris, P W *et al* (2010) *Marketing Metrics: The definitive guide to measuring marketing performance*, Pearson Education, Upper Saddle River, NJ

4   Farris, P W *et al*

5   Farris, P W *et al*

6   http://www.wpp.com/wpp/marketing/brandz/brandz-2013/ [accessed 11 October 2013]

7   http://brandirectory.com/league_tables/table/global-500-2013 [accessed 11 October 2013]

8   Reichheld, F (2003 [accessed 11 October 2013]) One number you need to grow, *Harvard Business Review*, December [Online] http://hbr.org/2003/12/the-one-number-you-need-to-grow/

9   Allen, D (in press) *Who? Oh... Wow!: The 55-minute guide to corporate branding*, Verb Publishing, Royston, Herts

10   Treacy, M and Wiersema, F (1995) *The Discipline of Market Leaders*, Addison-Wesley, Wokingham

03 Defining your brand

'Would you tell me, please, which way I ought to go from here?'

'That depends a good deal on where you want to get to', said the Cat.

'I don't much care where –' said Alice.

'Then it doesn't matter which way you go', said the Cat.

'– so long as I get SOMEWHERE', Alice added as an explanation.

'Oh, you're sure to do that,' said the Cat, 'if you only walk long enough.'

(LEWIS CARROLL, *ALICE'S ADVENTURES IN WONDERLAND*)

Unlike wayward Alice, your organization does have to know exactly where it is going. In today's dynamic, always-on business environment, walking long enough in a direction hoping to reach your destination is probably not a very sensible strategy. This chapter focuses on how to discover and define the all-important direction of travel.

Current state of practice

The existing state of brand definition methods still remains largely in the arena of marketing and branding. Although the strategic process includes senior executive involvement (and ideally stakeholder and employee involvement), by and large most of the models being used today centre around some principles developed in the 1980s.

While there are numerous ways of staging the brand definition process (3 steps or 13), they all more or less amount to the same sequence of events.

1 Discovery

First, a research stage is required. Many favour the word 'Discovery'. In this discovery stage, you undertake a series of activities to uncover as much insight as possible into your organization and, importantly, its stakeholders.

Depending on your objectives, your stakeholders (see below)[1] may not be limited just to customers or employees of your organization. Often, efforts need to take into account other stakeholders who may be affected by changes in the way people inside your organization think and behave (and of course by the products or services they provide).

These can include:

Your organization

- senior executives and leaders;
- business and people managers;
- employees – particularly new starters (and their families and friends);
- contractors (and their families and friends);
- former employees (alumni);
- future (potential) employees.

Other organizations

- outsourced functions (HR, IT, etc);
- suppliers;
- partners;
- regulators and government and related bodies;
- media and analysts.

The broader community

- the investment community;
- shareholders/investors;
- environmental and corporate responsibility interests.

Your customers/consumers or clients

- potential customers or clients;
- current customers or clients;
- past customers or clients.

Your competitors

- direct 'traditional' business competitors;
- non-traditional and indirect competitors;
- competitors for talent.

What this discovery phase seeks to uncover is the answer to some pretty simple questions, the most important of which is: 'Why?'

- Why should a customer consider buying your product or service?
- Why would a candidate want to come and work for you?
- Why are you relevant and different from your competitors – for business and for talent?
- Why (or how much) do people trust what you say – and why not?
- What would most need to change for them to consider your company?
- What are the alternatives to your organization, and what makes them interesting and relevant?

The typical approaches to engaging them include guided interviews, focus groups, workshops, virtual events with your own executives, leaders, managers and a cross-section of staff to generate their perspectives and contribution. Generally these interviews should be done by a third party to ensure robust conversation and an independent or at least plausibly objective view.

Particularly with customers and consumers, additional insight is often generated through data mining and analysis, focus groups and surveys, net promoter score and a raft of social media monitoring/sentiment monitoring which can provide information to add to the mix.

Positioning

The process also should include an all-important positioning exercise. We touched on positioning in the previous chapter, and we'll talk more about positioning in greater detail in Chapters 8 and 12 to avoid duplication here. But simply put, given all of the information you manage to gain from the discovery stage, what is the best way to position your organization against its competitors in such a way that you make the most of what makes you authentic and relevant to your stakeholders? How do you differentiate who you are, what you do, why and how you do it?

2 Definition

The second stage is generally about taking all the insight generated in the discovery stage and turning it into some hypotheses around your positioning and how you may want to express it in words and images. Best practice suggests again going through the exercise of engaging with your stakeholders to evaluate and test a number of options to see which one is the most effective. It's at this stage where you will begin to form your brand 'platform' or model.

Brand models

These principles tend to focus on populating a 'brand model' that will serve as the guide to further development and expression of your brand. A quick online search for the terms 'brand models' can provide a number of examples for your assessment. There are as many brand models (or platforms) as there are brand consultants (indeed, probably more). Most of these models seek to define (although the terminology may vary significantly) some core elements that help provide guidance for the expression of your brand.

A 'brand essence' or 'brand DNA'

This very short statement seeks to clearly articulate what your brand stands for, when boiled down to its absolute essence. For example, a brand essence might be 'Quality' or 'Growth' or 'People first'. Putting on their shoe might make you feel 'Inspired'; riding their motorcycle might make you feel 'Liberated'.[2]

Brand attributes

What are the elements that combine to deepen the core idea in a way that clarifies it – generally, brand models seek to establish 3–8 attributes? Brand attributes might include things like innovative, sustainable, energetic and passionate.

Mobile phone maker Huawei's defined brand attributes

Customer-centric

We keep an unwavering focus on our customers, partnering with them and committing ourselves to meet their goals and needs. We rely on deep customer insights and continuous feedback to guide our priorities and influence the way we work.

Dedicated

We are passionate about the success of our customers, making every effort to meet our commitments. We measure our work against how much value we bring to customers. We strive to continuously improve ourselves, building our capabilities, our knowledge base, and our expertise.

Innovative

We proactively anticipate future trends and customer needs. Continuous innovation puts us directly on the cutting edge of technology. We generate new value through smart design and the integration of our products, services, and experiences.

Global

We operate on the world stage so that we can provide the best locally. We are actively engaged in communities; we learn from local cultures, recruit and develop local talent, partner with local suppliers, and customize our offerings for local tastes and needs.

Open

We are active listeners and contributors internally and externally. We always bring a unique point of view, listen to others' suggestions for how we can improve, and share knowledge and insights to help the industry and key stakeholders evolve and grow.

Trusted

We say what we do and do what we say, delivering on the promises we make to our customers and partners. We respect fair business practices and maintain the highest standards of information integrity and security. As a responsible corporate citizen, we actively promote the sustainable development of society, the economy, and the environment.

More information on Huawei, their brand promise and values and a breakdown of their services can be found on their website http://www.huawei.com

Brand promise

A brand promise is the statement that captures what the brand wants to stand for – the expression that comes to mind when people see or hear your name. It's sometimes called a 'brand positioning statement'. We're going to spend some time looking at Huawei as an example – there is a lot of easily accessible information about their brand and talent framework online. Huawei's brand promise is: 'Enriching life and improving efficiency through a better connected world.'

Brand values

Words that express how your brand 'behaves' provide a benchmark for its performance. Too frequently, brand values either conflict with, are separate from, or are not well aligned to stated corporate values.

> For a guide to the taxonomy of 'current state' brand definitions, you could do far worse than the comprehensive guide at
> **http://www.brandchannel.com/education_glossary.asp**.
> There is also a glossary at the end of this book.

Brand architecture

Brand architecture is a set of principles clarifying how an organization expresses the relative importance of different brands (or other elements) within its portfolio. At the most fundamental level, brand architecture shows how different brands – and the products or services they relate to – fit into the overall picture. It is the presentation of the way in which brands within a company's portfolio are related to, and differentiated from, one another (which helps stakeholders navigate the company offering). It relates to naming of products and services as well as sponsorships and other related marketing and communication activity/processes both internally and externally.

So, for example, a brand might go to market with just one name and identity (such as IBM). This is generally known as a 'monolithic brand' or 'umbrella brand' – in other words, IBM is IBM the world over and its products and services, which might well have their own sub brand names, will always be connected to IBM and its logo. Apple is a similar example.

An 'endorsed' brand is a product or service brand that has its own name, but is attached to an umbrella brand. There is usually a carefully considered relationship between the brand that endorses and the brand that is endorsed – one will always have greater prominence. The balance is selected based on the value of the brand being endorsed in the eyes of the end user/consumer, and the value of the brand providing the endorsement. Examples are Nestlé® KitKat® as a consumer product (a confectionery), or Silent Knight® by Honeywell (a security service). In each case the product or service brand has a reputation within its market, but is provided with additional equity through association with its parent brand.

There is also the sometimes confusing architecture category called 'house of brands' which refers to organizations such as Unilever and P&G who manage a broad portfolio of distinct individual brands, and the category called a 'branded house' in which all brands share a direct and explicit reference to an umbrella brand – but exist as a brand in their own right. A good example of this is Virgin – which is seen as Virgin Media, Virgin Atlantic, Virgin Music, Virgin Trains etc.

Architecture is important, and even in service organizations must be carefully managed and considered. For example, professional services firms often have a range of services that perform very different kinds of roles (for example, tax consulting, actuarial consulting, business analytics, litigation) but are aligned to the organization's overarching brand. It is essential that the way these services are expressed is carefully considered – do they get their own sub brand names, are they endorsed by the master brand, or are they simply descriptive?

The challenge

That all sounds like a pretty solid and clear set of tools: a promise, values and some attributes to help bring a brand to life and guide it. Some would argue, on the other hand, that this taxonomy and its surrounding ecosystem has wandered deep into the dark forest of 'management speak', 'marketing b.s.' or indeed 'brand babble' – which actually serves to conflict with the higher purpose of the organization, its services to its customers, and its relationships with its stakeholders and the people it employs, seeks to employ and no longer employs.

For example, while it might make perfect sense for marketing people creating a campaign to use brand values and attributes in their work, it makes much less sense for an employee to be presented with one set of 'corporate values' and another set of 'brand values' and then told which apply in different situations. We'll talk about this more later, but this is, in essence, the core premise of this book: you should really have one set that everyone works with.

Challenges with the current state

The idea of defining and clarifying the essence, attributes and other elements that help define, manage and defend brand value makes a lot of sense. It's hard to argue that you don't need a guide by which to steer how you influence perceptions of your reputation.

The problem is that a lot of these models emerged from consumer marketing approaches pioneered – very effectively and very innovatively – by P&G and Unilever in the 1980s. They have been broadly adapted for use in the corporate branding space. But P&G and Unilever, constant drivers of innovation, never really intended for these models to be used outside the context of a brand manager trying to crack a new campaign for a consumer product.

In other words, these models are very good for developing and defending brand and marketing communications in the consumer and customer context. Where they start to be less effective is when they start being used for other purposes. Some would argue that they are no longer fit for the purpose of guiding critical decisions about reputation management in the fast-moving global economy of the internet and social media age, where audiences overlap and have access to a far greater range and depth of information, instantaneously.

In the old world, functions could, with reasonable confidence, 'own' a certain segment of the stakeholder universe. For example, traditionally corporate communications as a function 'owned' media and investors as an audience; marketing and sales 'owned' attracting and converting potential customers; HR 'owned' the employee in terms of hiring, firing, pay and rations; internal communications 'owned' the listening to and sharing of information with employees; the business 'owned' the provision of product and service; and so on.

Looking at the above paragraph today, few would argue with it simply not matching the conventional wisdom of the world we operate in today. And yet the majority of organizations still seem to insist on functional ownership of the reputation management agenda. Cross-functional cooperation and coordination are fine, but few chief executives have the stomach to try to elevate any function into a genuine coordination role because of the political and operational Pandora's box it threatens to open.

There has always been debate about how to structure and manage corporate communications (and its relationship to other functions) and where various functional responsibilities should sit – across human resources, media relations, corporate social responsibility, brand, sales and marketing. And although different organizations manage this accountability in slightly different ways – sometimes internal communications sits in a corporate communications function, sometimes in the HR or marketing function – the lines between employees, stakeholders, customers, competitors, regulators and media have been seen to be relatively distinct. These relationships have also been relatively manageable within these distinct silos. They didn't require much cooperation internally to manage well.[3] But technology and social media have blurred or even erased these artificial dividing lines.

It's a truism to say that consumer power is growing due to greater transparency and access to information. What's less clear is whether the majority of organizations have made the connection between this growth in consumer/client influence and the way these organizations manage their stakeholder relationships (and indeed their businesses).

This shift in consumer power has a direct connection with employees, contractors, third-party relationships and how the organization operates in its environment. The model is no longer one where the organization sits at the centre and neat lines are drawn to discrete stakeholders.

Now, everyone is wearing a lot of hats. Consumers are now media producers – and very influential ones when it comes to an organization's reputation. Stakeholders and partners are now consumers – and, of course, influential media producers. These 'stakeholders' may not be who you think they are, and quite possibly are not who they used to be. Your supplier may be not only a competitor and a customer, but representing your brand and contributing, positively or negatively, to your reputation.

In most organizations today, the way these stakeholder relationships are managed is woefully inadequate to deal with the way these complex relationships have evolved and matured. This is precisely what is causing friction internally within organizations: Who is accountable for making sure that the customer experience is delivered? Product design ('The features are what people want')? Sales and marketing ('We need to increase turnover')? Human resources ('We need to attract great people, and keep the ones we have')? Call centre staff ('Whom do customers call when they have a problem')? Front of house or retail staff ('You never get a second chance to make a first impression')? Facilities ('A good retail and working environment is key')? Finance and credit control ('Have you seen the letter we send our valued customers when they miss a payment')? Digital and web teams ('We are the key touch point for our customers')? The executive suite ('It's all about leadership')?

The answer, of course, is that *all* of these people build and protect your reputation, in one way or another. The problem is, if the organization hasn't sorted itself out, the person bearing the brunt of poor organizational design and process is – you guessed it – the customer, client or consumer.

And this brings us back to the point that an organization should only have one clear, easy to remember and use, set of ideas through which to drive its entire brand and reputation management agenda – in every single facet of its operations.

What's the problem?

If we take Huawei as our example (and it is a completely random example generated by my selecting the first good set of brand attributes I encountered in a web search), you quickly run up against this big, functionally oriented issue when it comes to reputation management. While the brand team have been polishing their attributes, the HR people have also been hard at work defining the culture, values and related attributes they seek to encourage, recognize and reward at Huawei.

So we have a brand with the above essence, promise and attributes. And here is what Huawei state are their:

Mission[4]

- enhancement of customers' interests;
- achieve sustainable growth and success;
- product roadmap driven by customer needs;
- build up a process-oriented organization.

Huawei also adds:

Core values[5]

- customer oriented;
- high performance culture;
- honesty and trust;
- team work;
- commitment;
- continuous improvement.

And Huawei clearly defines its culture[6] as:

- Pursuit – Huawei supports the pursuit of customers, and sets up far-reaching goals for employees and a down-to-earth working spirit.

- Staff – Everyone stands on the same starting line; Responsible and efficient people are the greatest asset of Huawei, and those who demonstrate outstanding capability and contribution will get promoted.
- Spirit – Being practical and realistic is the standard of Huawei behaviour – Sense of responsibility; Spirit of innovation; Devotion; and Team Work.
- Benefits – The benefits to customers, staff and contributors should be linked up; We never make a contributor suffer a loss; etc.
- Within the definition of culture, an additional set of core values:
  - obey regulations;
  - team work;
  - self-confidence;
  - hard work & creativity;
  - always in progress;
  - self-criticism.
- Cultural Collaboration principles:
  - to observe laws and regulations of the community as well as social morality and safeguard good relationships with the community;
  - to carefully fulfil one's own duties in a down-to-earth way;
  - to take initiative and communicate with others;
  - to actively seek help from others while selflessly helping others and jointly make progress through mutual help;
  - to be brave to criticize and self-criticize and constantly make progress;
  - to be cautious about one's lifestyle and strictly obey standards of local social ethics.

There is no doubt whatsoever that Huawei is a company that performs well, employs great people and wants to be a successful enterprise. Nothing in any of these statements is undesirable – in fact, it expresses a strong sense of teamwork, humility, ethics and a sense of innovation and excellence. But it would be challenging at any given moment for someone to say for sure what was most important when they are making a statement or taking a decision – other than 'It's about all of it.'

Yet Huawei is not alone by any stretch of the imagination – countless organizations face the same challenge and end up doing exactly the same thing.

One major UK retailer had no fewer than 23 separate categories of values/ attributes/behaviours for its people to juggle at one time (without referencing its separate employer brand proposition, or the additional, separate scorecard that leaders also needed to adhere to). Its HR director and chief marketing officer (CMO) didn't get along very well, it should be noted.

This is all an artefact of the industrial-age management thinking of Taylor, and of Henry Ford, which was completely suitable for the companies they oversaw and the products they produced in the context of the economics, technology and culture of their times. This is exactly what happens when executives fail to clarify and simplify – and lack the political will to force clarity and simplicity onto functions, primarily marketing and human resources, that have not been able (or willing) to align their agendas.

A closer look at the Huawei case study proves the point from the external supplier angle: each functional audience has been neatly aligned not only internally by function owners, but externally with specialist service providers. The supplier ecosystem has aligned itself to the internal functional ecosystem. So, for example, a series of suppliers (which is by no means unusual) from IBM to Hay Group and Towers Watson to PwC and others provide specialist expert support to the internal specialist experts along the value chain.[7] No doubt each has its own bespoke models and definitions that it applies to its work with the different internal functions.

You will often find a cottage industry of service providers all contributing to your reputation management efforts – brand, sales, marketing, corporate communications, social media, digital, employer branding and recruitment advertising, human capital communications, employee engagement, PR and media relations – all too often singing from different or poorly joined up hymn sheets. Not a great recipe for a great, harmonic performance.

This is not to say that there is anything remotely 'malicious' being done by functional leads, or their consultants, in arriving at a place where you have these disparate sets of values and visions and attributes and behaviours. Each is trying to deliver value and to apply their considerable expertise and technical skills to the task at hand – defining and shaping your reputation, and the processes by which you raise awareness, establish consideration, and deliver on the promises you make to people, customers and other stakeholders. But no one seems to have taken, or been given, the quite sensible job of saying: 'How do these all connect in a way that we don't end up with more then 50 sets of concepts to define what we ought to be doing every day when we come in to work, and the service we provide to our customers?'

There has to be a better way. There is – and we'll explore it in the third part of this book, starting in Chapter 8.

Meanwhile, let's park this thinking for the time being and continue our discussion about brand management as it is broadly practised today. The next chapter goes into the development of how you bring your brand to life visually and verbally. This is the third stage past *Discovery* and *Definition* that we'll call *Delivery* (brand people love alliteration) – approaches which, regardless of how you develop your brand definition, are truly essential to a successful outcome.

Notes

1   Keohane, K (2009) Advanced employee engagement, in *The Gower Handbook of Employee Communications*, Gower Publishing, London

2   Brandstoke [accessed 11 October 2013] *9 Criteria for a brand essence* [Online] http://www.brandstoke.com/2009/02/09/9-criteria-brand-essence/

3   Elements of this section originally published on 'Death to internal marketing' [Online] http://kevinkeohane.wordpress.com/2007/05/13/the-end-of-internal-communications-reprise/ [accessed 11 October 2013]

4   Huawei Technologies Company Limited, *HR Building & Culture Building in Huawei*, PDF available [Online] http://www.hruae.ae/hr-05/hcbh.pdf [accessed 11 October 2013]

5   See Note 4.

6   Note 4, paraphrased

7   See Note 4.

Brand delivery

04

> *And the Grinch, with his Grinch-feet ice cold in the snow,*
> *stood puzzling and puzzling, how could it be so? It came*
> *without ribbons.*
> *It came without tags. It came without packages, boxes or bags.*
> *And he puzzled and puzzled 'till his puzzler was sore.*
> *Then the Grinch thought of something he hadn't before.*
> *What if Christmas, he thought, doesn't come from a store.*
> *What if Christmas, perhaps, means a little bit more?*
> **(DR SEUSS, *HOW THE GRINCH STOLE CHRISTMAS*)**

All too often 'brand' is associated with logos and tags; guidelines, packages and, of course, boxes and bags. The Grinch discovered the essence of branding: emotional connection plays a very large role in an experience of an event, a product or a service.

These things are the expression of an organization's brand, and alongside your actual product or service they have a tremendous (and for strong brands disproportionate – you only need to look as far as any Apple product to appreciate the sentiment) influence on your reputation.

What's the point?

Your brand management is about one objective: using the assets at your disposal to have the maximum possible impact on building advocacy for your brand, internally and externally. Again, there are many models explaining this, but this advocacy is about building awareness, consideration and loyalty for your product and service. This advocacy results in your ability to command a premium price – because the stronger your brand, the less you need to spend on making people aware of it and convincing them to try it or to continue using it. It also means you will spend less on attracting better talent, will retain them longer and, believe it or not, probably pay them less than you would otherwise have to. If you are doing things that don't impact that objective, you should probably question why you are doing them.

How?

In 1989 Wally Olins published *Corporate Identity*[1] (he actually wrote 'The Corporate Personality: an inquiry into the nature of corporate identity' in 1978, long before that). It serves as the bedrock of many of the fundamentals of modern organizational branding. Olins described four key 'touch points' (or vectors) which combine to create your brand and brand experience.

These still apply, although many would argue that these touch points have evolved significantly in the 25 years that have since elapsed:

- *products and services*: the product or service that your organization provides and that people experience;
- *environments*: where the product or service is provided or created;
- *communications*: how you talk about and promote your product or service;
- *behaviours*: how you behave in creating and in delivering your product or service.

So once you have performed the 'discovery' and 'definition' work covered in the previous chapters, you need to set about making sure that what you have defined is effectively expressed across these touch points and across all of the stakeholder groups that we discussed in Chapter 3. We'll call this 'delivery', as mentioned earlier.

How do you go about delivering your brand?

In the previous chapter we looked at the sometimes-conflicting nature of organizational functions and their shared role in the creation and delivery of the products and services that define your brand.

In Chapter 7 we will explore an alternative method for creating an integrated approach to brand and talent management using a single set of core ideas that cross all functional boundaries. In this section, we'll look at good practices that still apply regardless of the way you have defined your brand platform or model. The good news is that if you have done your homework in the 'discovery' stage and then crafted a strong brand platform (however you have decided to articulate it) in the 'definition' stage, then the 'delivery' stage is made easier to manage coherently.

Guidelines

At some point in the process you will need to have created a set of guidelines by which to ensure that your brand is managed professionally. Generally, brand guidelines focus on the visual and verbal identity of an organization – that is, the logo, the typeface, the imagery and graphics used, and the kind of words and language that we employ. These are visualized and a set of rules provided that apply across a set of templates for things like advertisements, social media sites and websites, business cards, presentations, publications, stationery, retail and office environments, and so on.

The best guidelines are clear and succinct. All too often, however, guidelines become onerous, lengthy and nearly indecipherable as they attempt to cater for every possible eventuality.

With guidelines, the objective should really be about *coherence* – that is, when an end user is exposed to the environment, communication, experience or behaviour, it is unmistakable and recognizable as coming from your brand and your brand alone. What often happens, though, is that a less sophisticated – and generally less effective – objective is set: *consistency*. Consistency is important – clearly there should be rules to adhere to across the touch points – but should not be an end unto itself. Many brands fall into the 'consistency at all costs' trap and as a result underperform in terms of the impact they could generate from a more coherence-oriented approach. It is not unusual to have to remind a brand manager that their objective is to build a powerful brand that builds and defends reputation – not to ensure that everything they put out in their marketplace is 'consistent' when policed.

Increasingly, guidelines and other guidance documents include messaging and modulation of tone of voice across both media and messages. The best guidelines take your core brand idea and allow it to 'breathe' – the idea of flexibility within a framework, extending the idea appropriately for different sectors, audiences and cultures. Getting the balance between what is immutable and what can be modulated is as much art as science, and requires a deep understanding of the markets and cultures – internally and externally – across which your brand must operate.

Customer and user experience

Much of the touch-point approach can be best defined and managed through the process of thinking through the different stages an individual is likely to go through when they experience your brand. Although it is often viewed solely through the consumer, client or customer lens, this applies to all of your stakeholders and should be mapped accordingly (Table 4.1).

TABLE 4.1   Things to consider

Who	What is the experience you want to provide and how does that experience ultimately translate into advocacy for your brand?
Potential customer/client/consumer Existing customer/client/consumer Past customer/client/consumer Potential employee Existing employee Past employee Potential investor/analyst Existing investor/analyst Past investor/analyst Journalist Government agency or regulator NGO or academic institution Competitor Community	• Where, how and when are they likely to encounter your brand? • What are they looking for and what are the questions they are likely to ask, the information they are likely to seek? • What are you saying and how are you saying it? • What is the sequence of events they are likely to experience – and how can you help create, manage and curate that experience? • What is most likely to delight them? • What is most likely to irritate, offend or disenfranchise them? • How easy are you making it for them?

FIGURE 4.1 Variations on the 'customer lifecycle marketing' theme

01 BRAND AWARENESS	02 BRAND CONSIDERATION	03 BRAND SELECTION	04 BRAND EXPERIENCE	05 BRAND ADVOCACY	06 BRAND DEPARTURE
Your reputation as an organization in the mind of your marketplace	Your potential customers or clients include your brand in their consideration set when looking at alternatives	The first experience the customers have when they decide to purchase/use/ consume your product or service	The ongoing experience of your product or service	The level of advocacy (best expressed as a net promoter score) for your brand	The experience customers have when they stop using your brand for whatever reason

User experience mapping

Similarly, you can think through your customer's experience of your brand by looking at what stage of the 'customer lifecycle' they are at. As with many of these things, a simple web search will lead you to a number of variations on the 'customer lifecycle marketing' theme, but for our purposes we will use those shown in Figure 4.1.

1 Brand awareness

Your potential customers and other stakeholders have to be aware of your brand in order to form any sort of opinion regarding it. Once they have any level of awareness regarding your brand, they will form some sort of opinion – positive, neutral or negative – about it. Brand awareness-raising communications therefore play an important role.

2 Brand consideration

Your potential customers, if sufficiently positive about the relative merits of your brand, may include you in their 'consideration set'. They may use a number of resources to assess your brand's merits – a lot of which is completely outside your control. While you will have made efforts to influence perceptions about your brand through your website, communication and marketing, advertising, promotion, signage and so on, customers will access much more information about your brand. They will use websites, press articles, blogs, social media, word of mouth from friends and relatives and more to form an opinion about whether to consider you or not.

Once again, this supports the case for ruthless, relentless coherence in how you express your brand. If you are saying different things to different people in different places, your brand will be muddled and will lack clarity and coherence.

3 Brand selection (preference)

The initial impression of your brand is critical once the customer has decided to use your brand for the first time. This experience is often under-represented in customer lifecycle models. It is very easy to lose a customer at this stage by overpromising and under-delivering – and, though it's a cliché, 'You never get a second chance to make a first impression.' A great example of this is companies who have integrated their packaging design as part of the customer experience (Apple were pioneers of this: opening their product became part of what made the experience exciting and fun – before you even held it in your hands!). Similarly, services businesses should excel at this and make you feel welcome and valued. Reinforcing your brand post-purchase is absolutely essential.

Think about how you feel when you've decided to purchase something or use a service, and the next communication you receive is an invoice with no welcome or thank you.

4 Brand experience

Although the entire lifecycle is really the totality of the brand experience, for the sake of simplicity we'll use this term to cover the brand in 'day-to-day use'. This is the performance of the product or service, the support and customer service, its reliability, the ease (and pleasure) of use, the emotions that using it – and being seen to use it – evoke.

If you are delivering on your promise, what you claimed your brand would do and what it would feel like, you will have very happy customers.

5 Brand advocacy

A positive brand experience is important – but the real goal is to translate existing customers into advocates. In Chapter 3 we talked about the 'net promoter score' and this is where you want to turn as many customers into advocates (with as few detractors) as possible. The cost of acquiring a customer is high in most sectors (at least 6–7 times the cost of retaining one, according to Bain & Company), so once you have customers it is essential not just to satisfy them but to convert them into passionate advocates for your brand.

For some brands and sectors, of course, this is harder than in others – but in any event, regardless of the contribution your brand makes to your ability to charge a premium and earn gross margin, creating advocates reduces your cost of brand management and increases your brand value.

6 Brand departure

At some point, customers leave your brand – and they leave for a variety of reasons. Some of this is within your control, and some of it isn't. What you'll notice is that your employees or representatives play a disproportionate role in this decision (Figure 4.2). It's for this reason that a more integrated approach to brand management and talent management is critical – and yet sometimes not managed accordingly by service organizations.

FIGURE 4.2   Why do people leave brands?

1%	7%	9%	14%	69%
DIE	MOVE AWAY	FIND A BETTER ALTERNATIVE	UNHAPPY WITH PERFORMANCE	TREATED POORLY BY AN EMPLOYEE

SOURCE: Amalgamated from Journal of Applied Psychology; Dan Kennedy; Brand Strategy Insider; et al.

Obviously, the talent component is critical – so critical, in fact, that we'll cover the employee lifecycle version of this later, in Chapter 5.

Later on, in Chapter 7, we will discuss the implications this sort of stakeholder experience mapping has on managing your reputation – particularly when you consider the cross-functional implications and challenges this presents. As you can imagine, some of the biggest implications are in the talent arena – where the 'behaviours' referred to as a touch point are encountered by all of these stakeholders.

SAY = DO

It has become a truism in the world of branding and brand management that the key to a successful brand is relatively simple: what you say as an organization simply has to match what you do as an organization at every touch point and with every stakeholder.

Great brands are very clear on why they exist, and they are very clear on what they stand for. They then invest a great deal of time, energy and resource to make sure that that idea is relentlessly and ruthlessly delivered across every touch point. They do what they promise.

Brands like these are the ones that end up with the greatest brand equity, and the greatest brand advocacy. They also are the brands that somehow manage to 'bank' enough goodwill that when they do falter – and at some point every brand does – their audiences are more likely to forgive them. Moreover, these brands are more likely to survive a major crisis than weaker brands – one needs only to look at examples like BP (which invested heavily in its global brand positioning and management for a decade before the Gulf of Mexico disaster – and managed to survive to tell the tale, despite the significant toll the episode has taken on the company's relationships with regulators, reputation and finances) and Tylenol (which famously removed its entire product range from shelves when tampering was discovered in their tablets in the 1980s and remains a market leader today).

Customer brand engagement

'Brand engagement' is often used as a term to describe efforts to go beyond 'communication' of the brand and form more of an attachment to the customer or other stakeholder. Using the touch-point approach, brands increasingly seek to create experiences related to the brand that are entertaining, enjoyable and rewarding. These can be events and sponsorships (Red Bull has become the master of this, as have some TOP and local Olympic sponsors and suppliers) or they can be bespoke events or experiences on and offline (for example, games on social network sites or interactive experiences).

There is still debate about the degree to which brand engagement activities, particularly in the online arena, enhance brand advocacy, as it can be difficult to measure. In 2010, Pepsi famously shifted significant marketing budget from advertising into what was probably the largest social media campaign at the time – generating 80 million votes for their 'Refresh' project, 3.5 million Facebook 'likes' and 60,000 Twitter followers... and subsequently saw market share in Dr Pepper and Pepsi fall by approximately 5 per cent each.[2]

Nonetheless, the idea is right if execution is still in its infancy in the online world: the objective is to engage external stakeholders (and your own people) in ensuring that the desired brand experience is delivered. P&G aimed to spend 35 per cent of its advertising budget on digital and mobile in 2014.[3]

Employee brand engagement

One of the biggest barriers to ensuring that your brand 'does' what it 'says' comes from lack of clarity internally. In general, the state of best practice is that it is essential to engage your employees in understanding, internalizing and delivering the right behaviours to drive brand engagement with other stakeholders.

Once again, the spectre of cross-functional ownership and collaboration rears its head. Who really 'owns' the engagement agenda when it comes to employees? Marketing can well argue that since it is accountable for defining, activating, building and defending the brand externally, it should be in charge of making sure that employees understand what they need to think, say and do. They also can be accused of 'internal marketing': some say that marketers lack the skill set required to manage effective communications with an employee audience, who it can be argued are a very different audience with a very different relationship to the business from that of a customer. And often they are seen to oversimplify things through overemphasizing customer focus.

Human resources can make the case that they are accountable for the effective and efficient acquisition, development and management of your employees – and therefore should be in the driver's seat when it comes to the 'brand engagement' agenda. But some would say that HR practitioners lack the communication and engagement capabilities required to engage effectively with audiences. They often are seen to be too transactional in mindset and too process focused – often overcomplicating things.

Internal communications might be seen as the logical owner and arbiter – after all, their job is usually to make sure that the right information is reaching the right people using the right channel at the right time. But it can be argued that the internal communications capability all too often acts as channel managers and 'packagers' who lack the broader business perspective and influencing skills required to navigate the balancing act effectively.

Cross-functional cooperation and collaboration has long been put forward as the solution to this dilemma – and in some cases, it is. It can work effectively. But it can also result in a watered-down, confused and all too often overcomplicated compromise – the classic camel, designed by committee. The Huawei example is, quite possibly, an example of how this solution can go wrong – a sensible enough arrangement, and an intention to do the right thing, but one in which it appears that there was no single decision-maker with the mandate, or the will, to cut through the complexity and craft a more sensible, single-minded, clear and effective synthesis.

Let's also be honest: organizations are political. The dynamics of personal influence, agendas, budgets, relationships and human nature are sometimes the biggest barrier to effective cross-functional cooperation and coordination. It is not unusual for the dynamics of inter-functional relationships to result in scuppering the business potential that effective brand and talent management should unleash for the organization.

And it is precisely how you can find yourself reading an employee manual replete with a signed-off and approved, functionally driven compromise that results in employees having to navigate and decipher upwards of 20 different things they need to be thinking about (a mish-mash of vision, mission, values, competencies, brand promises, attributes, behaviours, and models that fails to do anything other than confuse employees and make the leadership team look foolish).

We'll talk more about this in Chapter 7 – but first, let's move along from the world of brand and open the door for a tour of the world of talent management and engagement, after a quick look at the relevant and timely topic of social media.

Notes

1   Olins, W (1989) *Corporate Identity*, Thames & Hudson, London
2   *Wall Street Journal* (2011) With share down, PepsiCo will pump dollars into Pepsi marketing this year, 18 March
3   *Wall Street Journal* (2013) P&G Shifts marketing dollars to online, mobile, 1 August

Brand and social media

05

> *Social media allows us to behave in ways that we are hardwired for in the first place – as humans. We can get frank recommendations from other humans instead of from faceless companies.*
>
> **(FRANCOIS GOSSIEAUX)**

This is not a book about specific channels or social media. Nonetheless, the amount of conversation going on about the ins and outs of social media demands some coverage of its role, both internally and externally, in brand and talent management.

In its infancy as both an internal and external brand and talent set of media, it is evolving quickly. A Forrester research report found that:[1]

- 59 per cent of online consumers are active on social networking sites at least weekly, and one-third of online users have become a fan of a company or brand via social platforms like Facebook and Twitter;
- 92 per cent of marketing leaders believe that social media has fundamentally changed how consumers engage with brands;
- 23 per cent of online consumers visit social networking sites several times a day.

A study by InSight Consulting showed that:[2]

- 36 per cent of people have posted about a brand on social networks;
- 61 per cent of social networkers are willing to give feedback on brands and products;
- 42 per cent of social media users have had a conversation with a brand via social networks;

- only 15 per cent of social media users have been contacted by a company after posting a negative experience;
- 44 per cent of customers want to take part in the co-creation of products.

Earlier we touched on the profound changes in the way individuals and organizations communicate as a result of rapid changes to, and the accessibility of, communication technology. The fragmentation of channels, combined with the explosion in social media, has rewritten some of the rules and influenced nearly all of them. The Forrester report concludes that (quoting directly):

- Marketers accept that social media is now a fundamental part of brand building, but putting that theory into action is still a challenge as many struggle with how to use social engagement effectively. Social efforts do not represent a standalone solution and need the scale and consistency of paid and owned media.

- Brand building strategy and social strategy are inextricably intertwined. The fundamentals of brand building have not changed. Marketers must still forge an identity for the brand and communicate it across all consumer touch points to create a consistent brand experience. But in the 21st century, brands need to have a social story to leverage the emotional and persuasive elements that make offerings successful.

- There are three strategic roles social plays in brand building: Marketers must use social to serve their brand building objectives. It can help the brand:

  - build a relationship to become more trusted;
  - differentiate through an emotional connection to become more remarkable and unmistakable; and
  - nurture loyal fans to become more essential.

A Facebook white paper found strong correlation between consumer behaviour, social media presence and brand building: people are turning to other people like themselves for online insight into companies and products. In 2009, 12 per cent of people used social media as a resource in making purchasing decisions – this rose to 57 per cent in 2011.[3] This assertion is also supported by Edelman's annual Trust Barometer, which is a study of the degree to which informed publics trust a range of stakeholders from business to government to academics to 'people like themselves'.

According to Walmart CMO Stephen Quinn, 'Social media allows us to be part of a discussion with our customers at every stage of the relationship so we can better serve our customers.' Table 5.1 gives a short snapshot of social media for brand building.

Social media is social communication... technologically enabled

Social media is social communication that is technologically enabled. Mike Klein defines social communication as: 'The science, art and strategy of generating word of mouth, built on an understanding of why people communicate with each other.'

The longer version is: 'The seemingly spontaneous communication that takes place between individuals and groups within organizations and communities. In fact, it can be influenced through strategies that identify the key social networks within an organization, and what drives the behaviours of the key individuals connecting those networks.'[4]

Key to Klein's definition is understanding the composition of the communities themselves, and then understanding the motivation of those with the greatest influence within those communities. Klein advocates 'tribal' theory approaches to this effort, but whichever approach you use the starting point is clear.

While this is true and viable from an external 'social media for brand building' point of view, the most intriguing element in our discussion of the intersection of brand and talent management is where the employee interacts with other employees, and with external stakeholders, through the use of social media.

Social media as an internal tool

Clearly, there have been great advances in the use of social media platforms inside organizations. Some intranets have evolved social features (SharePoint is an example, although other platforms also accommodate social), while Yammer has created a 'Facebook for the Enterprise' approach that has also seen some success (as well as many challenges).

TABLE 5.1 A short snapshot of social media for brand building

Case studies	Source
Ford Ford was keen to explore new ways of promoting their 2011 Explorer and thus decided to reveal the new design on Facebook. The Manufacturer's agencies Team Detroit and Ogilvy 360 participated in creating an integrated campaign centred around Facebook. In order to build its Facebook community, Ford set up an alluring sweepstake that offered up a brand new Explorer as the top prize at stake once the Facebook page reached 30,000 fans. Further Like buttons were also linked to its other digital properties to enhance the buzz surrounding the campaign and drive connections. A 'Reveal' tab was then created on the Facebook page, enabling users to access an exclusive video showcasing the car similarly to how Autoshow productions would do. The tab also revealed a special Q&A session with Ford's CEO Alan Mulally. **RESULTS** Although the car was officially revealed to the industry and media in an event held in New York City, thousands of Ford Explorer Facebook fans throughout the world had also witnessed its introduction to the world. This was estimated to lead to a 104% increase in online shopping activity for the SUV, as opposed to the usual 14% shopping increase experienced after the broadcasting of a Super Bowl TV ad.	'Building Brands For The Connected World: A Social Business Blueprint' by Facebook, whitepaper, 2012, based on a commissioned study by Forrester Consulting, p 9

TABLE 5.1 *Continued*

Case studies	Source
Burt's Bees Burt's Bees also presents a successful use of Facebook for promotional purposes. The company launched its new Tinted Lip Balm on Facebook and encouraged consumers to engage with friends on discussing the product with each others. Instead of the message coming from Burt's Bees, the promotion was launched by users directly. The app allowed friends to select one of six shades of Lip Balm (Red Dahlia, Rose, Pink Blossom, Hibiscus, Tiger Lily, and Honeysuckle) to a Facebook connection with a message describing why that friend is a 'Natural Beauty'. **RESULTS** By allowing its consumers to take ownership of the direction of the storyline of its campaign, Burt's Bees encouraged brand awareness to grow in a genuine and authentic manner.	'Building Brands For The Connected World: A Social Business Blueprint' by Facebook, whitepaper, 2012, based on a commissioned study by Forrester Consulting, p 10
Red Bull The daredevil Felix Baumgartner completed an impressive stunt on Sunday October 14, when he rose more than 24 miles above the New Mexico desert in a 55-story thing helium balloon called the 'Red Bull Stratos' and jumped off it, reaching a speed of 830 mph in his nine-minute fall. He broke the record for both the height of the jump that he took, and the speed of his descent. Red Bull sponsored the event and it was broadcast worldwide, capturing the attention of around 8 million people. **RESULTS** The Red Bull Facebook page gathered around 216,000 likes and 30,000 shares in 40 minutes on its pictures. Another 32 million views were recorded on its Youtube account.	'How Red Bull creates Brand Buzz' *Harvard Business Review*

TABLE 5.1 *Continued*

Case studies	Source
Cadbury Google + also offers significant promotion opportunities for international brands. Cadbury is considered to be one of its earliest adopters and has a strong track-record of delivering successful campaigns through the platform. With a number of different initiatives under its belt, Cadbury was keen to explore new functions on the Google + platform. The communities feature which had just been introduced was cherry-picked to support its newest campaign. Google + communities allow users to network with people according to interests and shared passions. The communities can be set up as private groups, or open to the public which guarantees a greater level of engagement. Cadbury's inaugural 'Cakes & Baking – The Cadbury Kitchen' community was set up as it identified key content **RESULTS** • One of the top 100 communities on G+ • Over 20,000 members • Over 2,500 recipes posted • 20 interactions per post on average • 11 new recipes being formally developed as a result of the community member activity, all of which will be featured on the Cadbury.co.uk website	Google Case Study, Cadbury
LG The ultra-thin Super LED monitors by LG were launched by the company sponsoring a flash mob performance that was broadcasted on the world's largest LED screen. The video became a viral hit around the world. **RESULTS** • The video gathered over a million views in a few months.	http://www.somesso.com/casestudies/lg-1-million-video-views

The debate really isn't whether to have an intranet or a social media platform – it's really just making sure that the organization has provided its people with a platform that allows it to:

- enhance operational efficiency through promoting more effective knowledge sharing, information gathering, culture building and real-time communication;

- take advantage of the many benefits of mobility, enhancing the flexibility of the organization in accommodating work–life balance and 'digital workplace' initiatives;

- allow people to express themselves and bring their 'whole selves' to work as an inclusivity and diversity driver (as part of a 'tribe');

- promote the ability to engage and collaborate – vertically and horizontally – across the organization to reduce perceived unnecessary hierarchy and enhance co-creation and dialogue.

Social media as an external brand engagement tool

Many companies have been cautious in their adoption of social media when it comes to allowing their employees to access various platforms, let alone engage in company-related communication on them. The tide seems to be turning, however, as organizations begin to realize that their people can play a powerful, and positive, role in acting as ambassadors and advocates for the organization and its brand.

The most challenging transition that organizations must make once they have overcome the initial shock of sticking their toe in the waters of social media is to realize that they can't really seek to control the message. A good corollary is to remind sceptics that you can provide talking points, media training, coaching and endless briefing to any spokespersons you want, but when the camera rolls and the red light comes on, they can (and often do) say anything they want. They are not marionettes.

Many organizations adopt social media and then proceed to use it as another broadcast medium – firing off posts and tweets about their press releases or latest news. This only adds to the noise and isn't seen to be terribly useful, or effective. On the other hand, organizations that learn to empower their people, providing guidance – at all levels – to be responsible and accountable in their actions on social media (just as they are when they work in the office, on the shop floor, speaking to the media or at a conference) can reap the benefits.

When deployed appropriately, employees can act as brand advocates when it comes to media coverage, blogs, recruitment communications, customer service and a variety of other brand building, and defending, topics.

Certainly, the expectation of greater access to and use of social media tools will only grow as these tools increasingly enter the mainstream.

Summary

There is no shortage of information and opinion about the use of social media in brand building and employee engagement, so we won't labour the point here any further. The fact is, social media has been transformational in terms of the way people communicate with each other and with brands, and any organization would be foolish to ignore the opportunities (and challenges) it raises when it comes to their brand management and talent management efforts.

Notes

1   Stokes, T *et al* (2012) How social media is changing brand building, Forrester Research, 7 May

2   InSight Consulting (2011) *Social Media Around The World 2011*, September

3   Facebook Whitepaper (2012) *Building Brands for the Connected World: A social business blueprint*, based on a commissioned study by Forrester Consulting

4   Klein, M (2011) *From Lincoln to LinkedIn: The 55-minute guide to social communication*, Verb Publishing, Royston, Herts

PART TWO
Talent

The talent agenda

06

> *The real and effectual discipline which is exercised over a workman is that of his customers. It is the fear of losing their employment which restrains his frauds and corrects his negligence.*
>
> (ADAM SMITH)

Before, during and after people join you

Adam Smith said it hundreds of years ago: talent drives business outcomes. The 'talent agenda' covers the entire spectrum of activities you undertake relating to the people whom you employ to make your organization a success: how you make them aware of you; how you attract them to you; how you hire them and bring them aboard; how you manage them, inspire them, reward them, develop them; how you ensure that they know where you are headed and what their role is in helping to get you there; and how you handle it when they decide to move on. This agenda therefore covers a lot of ground and requires a very mixed set of skills and capabilities to manage effectively.

Employee engagement is an outcome that results from these combined activities relating to the effective identification, selection, onboarding, development, performance management and communication with an organization's talent. In other words: if you can attract the right people, bring them aboard, encourage them and empower them to develop their careers and experience high performance, then they will be more 'engaged'. They will be happier, more productive, more loyal, deliver discretionary effort, stay longer and become brand advocates.

My definition of employee engagement is:[1]

The degree to which employees care about, and are willing to go the extra mile
for, their customers, their colleagues, their companies and their communities in
the context of their work.

A bit of the history

As a business management discipline, the idea of 'employee engagement'
emerged from crossover between cutting-edge internal communications thinking and organizational development ideas coming together. Probably the most
significant inflection point was in March 1994 when HBR published an intriguing article by Heskett *et al* about the experience that US retailer Sears
had when it purposefully linked employee engagement metrics, customer
service metrics, and profit.[2]

Based on some previous work done by Reichheld and Sasser[3] which indicated that a 5 per cent increase in customer loyalty can produce profit increases from 25 to 85 per cent, Hesket *et al* went on to make the link from
customer loyalty to employee engagement (then measured as 'satisfaction')
– and found with Sears that a 5-unit increase in employee engagement
predicted a 1.3-unit increase in customer satisfaction which could be statistically linked to a 0.5 per cent increase in revenue. Given that the worlds of
both HR and employee communications, at the time, were struggling to
demonstrate to the C-suite the strategic business value of their functions,
this was manna from heaven: they now had hard data to demonstrate the
value of their efforts to engage employees.

Subsequent studies have replicated and validated this model and its overall
findings. Gallup's data[4] indicate very specific and measurable benefits arising
from highly engaged workforces, including:

- customer ratings;
- profitability;
- productivity;
- turnover (for high-turnover and low-turnover organizations);
- safety incidents;
- shrinkage (theft);
- absenteeism;
- quality (defects).

The Gallup data (and related studies tend to support the general findings)
show that businesses in the top quartile in employee engagement out-

performed bottom-quartile ones by 10 per cent on customer ratings, 22 per cent on profitability and 21 per cent on productivity. Work units in the top quartile also saw significantly lower turnover (25 per cent in high-turnover organizations, 65 per cent in low-turnover organizations), shrinkage (28 per cent) and absenteeism (37 per cent), and fewer safety incidents (48 per cent) and quality defects (41 per cent).[5]

Other Gallup research found that:

> Workgroups that score above the median on employee engagement **or** above the median on customer engagement were 1.7 times more financially effective than units that score below the median on both measures. But workgroups that scored above the median on **both** customer and employee engagement were, on average, 3.4 times more financially effective than the units ranking in the bottom half on both measures.[6]

The Corporate Leadership Council (CLC) has also undertaken significant research[7] in this area. Their model is similar to the service profit chain.

CLC engagement model

The model is shown in Figure 6.1.

FIGURE 6.1   The Corporate Leadership Council's model of engagement

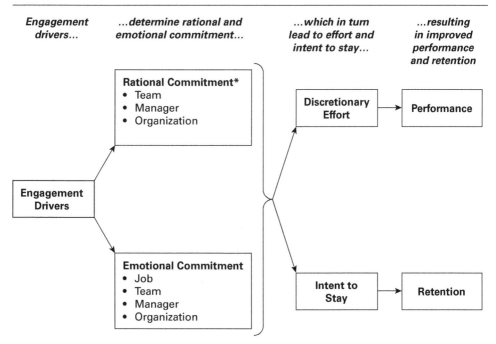

Other CLC findings are also enough to grab one's attention – their data show that not only effective engagement, but effective management of the external talent brand drives significant business benefits demonstrated in this model.

CLC's HR EVP framework

The model is shown in Figure 6.2.

There is a large bank of research that has found similar results to the service profit chain model, Gallup and other studies (including, for example, the TowersWatson Global Workforce Study... a list of resources is provided at the end of this book).

Just as importantly, the so-called 'War For Talent' is still alive and well, even in a time of economic lethargy. Businesses the world over are still constrained in their performance and growth aspirations by the inability to get the talent they need to achieve their goals. PWC's global CEO survey[8] finds:

- 58 per cent of CEOs are concerned about the availability of the key skills they need.

- At the same time, 23 per cent of all CEOs (40 per cent in Western Europe) plan head-count reductions – meaning they clearly need the people they still retain to deliver as only fully engaged employees can.

- 57 per cent of CEOs will improve their focus on ethical behaviour due to the lack of trust in their marketplaces.

FIGURE 6.2   The Corporate Executive Board Company's model

- 77 per cent of CEOs plan a rethink in the way they engage talent. 'But CEOs have told us the same thing for the past six years. This suggests that the changes they've made aren't working. Clearly, a change in the established approach to talent strategy is needed.'

- 79 per cent said that the most effective way of developing leadership in their organizations was to involve managers below board level in strategic decision making – but only 34 per cent actually do it in practice.

- A third of CEOs believe that 'pay for performance' models aren't working.[9]

So in essence the argument is simple. There are significant business benefits of getting employee attraction, retention and engagement right:

- Total shareholder return/Earnings per share tends to be higher in organizations with engaged employees.

- External brand equity, customer reach and customer loyalty are higher in organizations with engaged employees.

- Attraction, performance and retention of high-performance people are more effective and efficient in highly engaged organizations.

- The cost of recruiting and retaining that high-performing talent is lower in organizations with engaged employees and a strong talent brand in the marketplace.[10]

Why do organizations struggle, then?

Therefore, the issue is no longer one of having to find the evidence with which to convince an organization's leadership to invest in 'engaging its employees'. If the business case is so obvious and the world is awash with 'best practices' in internal communications, talent attraction, human resource management and employee engagement, why is it that so many organizations struggle to attract, engage and retain the talent they need?

It is a question of:

- How – what is the best way to achieve a strong culture, and reputation for, of highly engaged people?

- Who – should lead the effort in the first place?

Once again we come back to the issue of a functionally driven management mindset addressing a challenge that is inherently cross-functional and multidisciplinary by its very nature. There are a number of social, economic and technological reasons why rapid and large changes in the external market have outstripped (or at least stretched to near-breaking point) the ability of old-world silos of HR, Marketing, and Communications to deal effectively with the challenge.

The first big shift, not surprisingly, has been the rise of the internet, social media, transparency and access to information on an unprecedented scale. An organization used to be able to communicate to 'captive audiences' without needing to worry about mixed messages because the media, and the audiences, didn't cross over so much. But this is no longer the case. Everything you say is more or less visible to all of your audiences, both internally and externally.

The second big shift, related to the first, is media fragmentation. Content has been separated from the means of distribution, so channel ownership – while cheaper and easier than ever – is no longer a prerequisite for reaching any given audience with any given content.

The third big shift, amply demonstrated every year by Edelman's Global Trust Barometer,[11] is that increasingly informed people, all over the world, no longer trust what companies, CEOs, executives and governments say to them.

If you line up these three external dynamics against the internally focused, functionally driven mindset, it's pretty clear that a solution that goes beyond 'cross-functional working' is in order. Having said that, cross-functional working is not a bad place to start – so let's take a quick look at what is, arguably, the state of play in most organizations today.

Functional ownership of the brand and talent agenda

Table 6.1 lists a number of 'friction points' relating to the brand and talent agenda.

TABLE 6.1 Functional ownership of brands

Issue/task	Functional ownership	Friction points
Recruiting/ Talent acquisition	Human Resources (Talent Acquisition)	• The trend for HR departments to create standalone 'Employer Brands' to help differentiate in the talent marketplace – sometimes resulting in potential marketplace confusion relating to organizational brand and marketing messages
Internal communications and employee engagement	Varies, but typically: • Human Resources • Corporate Communications	• 'Employee engagement' is such a broad topic it touches on virtually every aspect of the workplace • In this context, even limiting it to 'business as usual' culture, behaviour and performance-related issues is still too broad • Internal communications sometimes seen as separate, depending on organization's definition of 'engagement' (so you can have one team 'communicating' and another team 'engaging') • Assigning 'ownership' to an individual function becomes problematic and political • HR models sometimes clash with marketing and communications models
Employee brand engagement	Brand/Marketing	• Customer/client-focused messaging seen to conflict with, or compete with, other employee engagement and communications efforts • Brand and marketing models sometimes clash with HR models

TABLE 6.1   *Continued*

Issue/task	Functional ownership	Friction points
Alumni relations	Varies, but typically: • Corporate Communications • Marketing • Human Resources	• Alumni are both an HR audience from a recruiting and reputation standpoint, and a marketing audience from a business standpoint
Sales, marketing, advertising, media relations	Corporate Communications, Marketing	• Fragmentation of media and consolidation of audiences have made all of these audiences more accessible – in other words, the talent market sees everything the business market sees and vice versa
Internal business initiatives	By function	• For example – new brand positioning; global mobility programme; reorganization; new strategy; new leadership; acquisition/merger • All require unprecedented levels of alignment and collaboration not seen in previous decades
And so on...		

Of course, many organizations do a good job of managing these frictions and perform exceptionally well. But there are just as many who fail to achieve their potential because of their inability to manage cross-functional tasks successfully, efficiently or even effectively. All too often, function agendas seem to overshadow organizational agendas – sometimes for good reasons, but sometimes not.

> ### And the winner is...
>
> It is interesting to note that many of the 'award winning' case studies one encounters in the 'talent and engagement' space prove the point: they are often awarded based on (or through) a functionally oriented organization or association – for example the Chartered Institute for Personnel Development (CIPD); the Chartered Institute for Public Relations (CIPR); the International Association of Business Communications (IABC); the Institute of Internal Communications (IoIC); Design Effectiveness Awards; Brand awards; and so on. While some of these awards include categories for a range of cross-functional types of engagement and communication activities, most bring with them the biases and perspectives of the sponsoring organization or association. There are relatively few examples of genuinely integrated awards and best-practice-sharing frameworks – wouldn't it be great if CIPR and CIPD joined forces with IoIC to host an integrated programme?

Even within the realm of employee engagement one can find inter-functional competition or friction. There are examples where organizations have actually separated 'internal/employee communication' as a communication function, and 'employee engagement' as an HR function. This duplication of effort is motivated by a desire to lock organizational development and performance into the talent management and engagement agenda, but it is taking the idea in precisely the wrong direction. Just as in the external communication and engagement world the watchword is integration, so inside organizations the same is true.

In my opinion, 'engagement' is the *outcome* of what happens when you manage how you engage with employees in an integrated manner, not by trying to split out different pieces of the puzzle across different functions. That's – to quote Microsoft's Dave Coplin – the old-world piecework approach of 'process standardization... if we want to break down how to make cars, let's break down that process into a series of widgets. "I no longer make cars, I make widgets." '[12] That only contributes to employees receiving an increasingly disconnected series of communications and initiatives from a new and expanded range of internal functional communicators. It's like pouring water on a drowning man.[13]

But before we get to the integrated approach, let's get some of the foundational elements out of the way. The next chapter will cover some of the basics around good practices in employee engagement, using the idea of the employee lifecycle (or employee experience) to cover the range of disciplines and activities required.

Notes

1   Adapted from Keohane, K (2007) *The Gower Handbook of Employee Communication*, Gower Publishing, Aldershot; and *The Talent Journey*, Verb Publishing, Royston, Herts, 2009

2   Heskett, J *et al* (1994) Putting the service–profit chain to work, *Harvard Business Review*, March

3   Reichheld, F and Sasser, W E Jr (1990) Zero defections: quality comes to services, *Harvard Business Review*, September–October

4   Sorenson, S (2013) How employee engagement drives growth, *Gallup Business Journal*, June

5   Sorenson, S (2013)

6   *Gallup Management Journal* (2008) When engaged employees meet engaged customers, February

7   Corporate Leadership Council (2004) Driving performance and retention through employee engagement

8   PWC (2013 [accessed 11 October 2013]) 16th Annual Global CEO Survey [Online] http://www.pwc.com/talentchallenge

9   It is probably worth a look at Dan Pink's *Drive* and its exploration of motivation – that is, pay for performance can actually diminish results when the task is complex and cognitive in nature, rather than routine. See Pink, D (2011) *Drive: The surprising truth about what motivates us*, Canongate Books, Edinburgh. For a quicker explanation, see the superb animation at http://www.youtube.com/watch?v=u6XAPnuFjJc [accessed 11 October 2013]

10 Keohane, K (2010) *The Talent Journey*

11 http://www.edelman.com/insights/intellectual-property/trust-2013/ [accessed 11 October 2013]

12 The full interview is in Chapter 17

13 A little-known R&B song by James Carr which reached up to 23 on the R&B charts in 1966

Engaging talent[1]

07

> *My grandfather once told me that there were two kinds of people: those who do the work and those who take the credit. He told me to try to be in the first group; there was much less competition.*
>
> **(INDIRA GANDHI)**

It is a journey

Engaging with talent happens long before people join your organization and should continue after they leave it. So by its very nature it has always been, and will always be, a task that requires a multidisciplinary, cross-functional mindset. With the proliferation and fragmentation of media, and the overlapping of a variety of disciplines in the conversation that organizations have with future, current and past talent in an increasingly complex stakeholder environment, this holistic view becomes all the more critical.

Looking at the entire lifecycle an individual goes through in their relationship with your organization, one thing should become very clear: specialist expertise in any one aspect of the conversation (or journey) is essential. But what is even more important is the intent and the ability to manage the different links and relationships among these stages to create a cohesive, coherent story. Engaging people happens within the context of your organization, its marketplace for both customers and talent, and the varying agendas of individuals and indeed your competitors for talent – so it is a complex, adaptive system at that. A change, a communication, an action within any single part of this interrelated system can have unintended and unexpected effects in other parts of the system. Not only that, but there is usually a significant amount of duplication that can be avoided and efficiencies gained by a more joined-up and holistic approach.

It's for this reason that many employee engagement, organizational change, HR and other transformation efforts sometimes fail to achieve their desired objectives. By overly focusing on a single part of the spectrum, they may well be causing disconnection, noise, confusion or bigger problems in other parts of the system. Organizations are rife with this – employees are all too often on the receiving end of disconnected messages from marketing, IT, HR, finance, the executive suite, their manager, the change communication team and 'business as usual' internal communications. And for every organization that has managed to put in place a structure and discipline to manage it, there is another creaking under the weight of this information overload.

The real challenge is to ensure that the organization's leadership alights on a simple, single set of core ideas that it wants to ensure everyone focuses on. This is not an easy task and could easily take up a book of its own. But it is the key to success at managing the complexity of not only bringing your brand to life, but also in creating an impactful and resonant talent engagement strategy that delivers all of the good things we discussed in the previous chapter.

This simple, single idea or set of ideas can come from any number of places – I propose what I believe to be a very effective one in Chapters 8–12. Perhaps it is your Vision, or your Values. Perhaps it is your Strategy, or your Mission. It could be many things – but the key is to make sure that there is one big idea or thought that everything else aligns with and takes its cue from. Remember the Huawei example from Chapter 3? Many organizations, including some which nevertheless manage to perform very well, end up in a similar place. Imagine how they would perform if they had greater focus on one big idea or set of ideas instead of 20!

Once you have this idea, it becomes much easier and productive to begin to align the many and varied functional requirements to delivering against it throughout the employee lifecycle.

The employee lifecycle

The employee lifecycle (sometimes called the employee journey, or experience) is a simple way of thinking about the experience people have with your organization from an employment perspective – before, during and after their association with you (Figure 7.1).

It starts off with their level of awareness of your brand – your reputation in their minds of your business. It then covers their perception of you as an employer. Assuming they want to work for you, it then covers their (and

FIGURE 7.1   The employee lifecycle

01 BRAND	02 TALENT BRAND	03 RECRUITMENT EXPERIENCE	04 JOINING EXPERIENCE	05 WORK EXPERIENCE	06 DEPARTURE EXPERIENCE
Your reputation as an organization in the mind of your talent market	Your reputation as an employer in the mind of your talent market	The influence you seek to have and the experience you create for potential employees	The experience you create for new employees	The experience you create for existing talent	The experience you create for people who leave, regardless of the reason

your) efforts to agree to work with each other. Then, once they have signed on the dotted line, it is about their experience of joining you, their ongoing induction, training, compensation, reward, recognition, career opportunities, your culture – basically the entire range of experiences they have as employees. And at some stage they will decide they no longer want to work with you, and they will decide to leave. Your relationship with them lasts long after they have left your employment.

We'll break the employee lifecycle into each of these segments and talk about them in more detail – but the question you might want to be thinking about as we do this is: How well does my organization manage this as a cohesive process? Who does what, when, how and why? Is it aligned and consistent and is there a clear thread that connects the whole experience? Or are there areas where what we 'say' and what we 'do' could very easily have come from a completely different organization? Chances are, like most organizations, you will have a bit of both – but asking the question can help you focus on where you might be bleeding important value and alignment at a critical part of a person's employment experience with you.

1 Your brand

While we have already covered that your brand is the sum total of everything your audience thinks, feels and believes about your organization – including what you mean to customers, employees and other stakeholders – to a certain degree many people will not naturally or automatically think about you as an employer. So for this reason we have included this touch point for the purposes of this discussion.

So the first thing that people will encounter about you is your brand – your reputation. This is something influenced by marketing, advertising,

PR, what the media says about you, your offices, signage, websites, delivery vehicles, employees, former employees, customers and former customers, regulators and even competitors – a whole universe of stakeholders.

People have become much more sophisticated consumers of media and information as technology has advanced and channels proliferated. They no longer just consume media; many (if not most) now produce it. The touch points have become far more numerous and your audiences have both greater choice and greater voice.

Great companies find that this touch point is already imbued with their reputation as an employer – unprompted questions will generally include things like 'they have great people' or 'it is a great place to work'. In many cases these companies include some form of employment-related messaging in their consumer or customer messaging.

The point is that, ultimately, every organization has one overarching reputation or brand that it seeks to create, build and defend. Your reputation as an employer is a critical component of this, and one which no organization can long afford to neglect in the talent-hungry marketplace of today. So brand, marketing, communications and HR all have a role to play and a stake in the end results.

2 *Your talent brand*

A 2012 LinkedIn White Paper, 'Why Your Employer Brand Matters', found that a strong *employer brand* (as indicated by an individual having a positive impression of a company) is twice as likely to be linked to job consideration as a strong *overall brand*. So this next stage, when a person considers working for your organization, matters. It's an important component of your brand overall, and it comes to the fore when it's being viewed in the context of the job seeker – and both existing and past employees, who have significant influence on it.

Like your overall brand, your reputation as an employer isn't fully within your control. The best you can do is influence it positively through clarity, consistency, coherence and – yet again – delivering on what you say. What you say, how you say it and where you say it – and what you do, how you do it, when and where you do it – have significant influence. Whether it's online, in your retail environment, in your offices and workspaces, your advertising, articles in the press, investor relations, word of mouth, social media, internal communications, employee engagement, HR policies and practices, change management – all of these things combine to create a perception of what your organization is like as a place to work.

It's also important to be clear on terminology – there are many confusing variations on this theme. The way I recommend talking about it, if you need to rely on specialist terms, is as follows. Your 'employer brand' or 'talent brand' is your reputation in the talent market that you seek to influence. It exists in the minds of your audience. You don't craft an 'employer brand' as a project – it is the outcome of a variety of activities.

On the other hand, you *do* craft how you want to be perceived – your 'employ*ment* value proposition' or 'EVP'. Some call it an employ*er* value proposition (too focused on the organization's perspective) and some call it an employ*ee* value proposition (too focused on the individual employee). So for that reason I recommend keeping it balanced since it is a reciprocal arrangement shared by the two parties. It's the promise of the experience you will share as employer and employee.

There are many providers of so-called 'employer branding' services who seek to help refine and express an organization's EVP in an effort to influence their talent brand. Often these are commissioned by HR departments – ideally with some coordination and collaboration with marketing and brand management. The ultimate aim is to express what the employment experience is within the context of the overall brand, and to do so in a manner that is authentic to your organization; relevant to your audience; and differentiating from your competitors for talent:

- *Authentic*. It has to be true to the reality of the organization and its culture. As with your brand and reputation management efforts, saying one thing but doing another is the quickest way to destroy brand value. It doesn't matter if you come up with something relevant and differentiating if it simply isn't reflective of reality.

- *Relevant*. It has to be interesting and compelling to your audience. There is always something interesting about an organization and its culture, regardless of its size, sector and location. It's no good having something true and distinctive if it is just not appealing to your desired talent.

- *Differentiating*. It has to be clearly distinctive from alternatives. It shouldn't be different for the sake of it – the difference has to be meaningful. And it's no good having something that is authentic and relevant if all of your competitors for talent say the same thing.

One of the risks of 'employer branding' efforts is that they are, in reality, either over-exaggerated recruitment marketing campaigns with a 2–3-year shelf life, or, alternatively, they try to create a 'sub brand' or vanity brand for

HR that actually can conflict with, and cause confusion with, your overall reputation management efforts. Once again, it's critical to engage with the widest possible range of stakeholders when developing your employment value proposition.

The other risk is looking at the employment value proposition as applying to the external audience only. It should instead cover the entire employee experience. Since your organization is not only promising an experience externally to the talent marketplace, it has to be delivering on that promise in everything it says and does internally and with alumni. It is part and parcel of managing and engaging the talent an organization already has – and seeks to develop and retain.

Chapters 8–12 propose a robust way to help ensure definition, alignment and effective implementation of your EVP.

3 Recruitment experience

How you attract and assess potential talent is a critical part of delivering on your EVP and positively influencing your talent brand. With talent shortages proving to be a persistent challenge and barrier to growth even in times of economic uncertainty the world over, getting this right is no longer a back-office function. It is a critical driver of performance and growth.

What is critical to understand is that your talent acquisition strategy should not only be about finding candidates – it needs to be about finding the right candidates. If you get your EVP right, a big part of its role is actually to deflect interest from candidates who are not right for your organization, and who by entering your talent acquisition process will consume your time and resources. The ultimate goal is fewer applications of higher quality.

Companies with a weaker employer brand report a cost per hire that is almost double that of companies with a strong employer brand.[2]

The talent marketplace is an increasingly complex ecosystem. The traditional economic assumption that talent markets are local is being turned on its head. It's essential, therefore, that your recruitment experience is completely integrated and that you are managing it across as many relevant and effective touch points as possible. This includes:

- your website (not just your careers site);
- your careers site (not just your website);
- social media presence;
- recruitment advertising on and offline;

- job boards;
- PR and media relations;
- employee referral;
- recruitment agency management;
- university relations;
- ... and more.

Every communication relating to talent (and potentially relating to talent) needs to be aligned to your brand and your EVP – so that, wherever you are interacting with a stakeholder who has the potential to influence your reputation as an employer, you are forming a coherent, credible, clear picture. If you are telling different stories to different stakeholders in different times and places, it will be apparent to the talent market – and will reduce your effectiveness in attracting the best. How you go to the market for talent speaks volumes to who you are as an organization and how you manage your business.

Also be very aware of the people you do not offer employment to. They too have an influence on your reputation. Think of every applicant as a potential brand advocate – even those you say 'no' to should have a positive experience and, while they might not become a net promoter, you can at least prevent them from being a detractor. Keep a close eye on your recruitment agencies when it comes to this – they can often cause significant damage without your even knowing about it.

> This is not just true for the recruitment of graduate entry-level talent or experienced hires. Organizations are often good at tackling those challenges and then failing to apply even the most basic brand and cultural filters to the talent they bring in at the executive level. For some interesting insights into this, and the world of executive recruiting, read the interview with Bob Benson, one of the most respected executive recruiters on the face of the planet, in Chapter 15.

4 Joining experience

Just as with a new customer, 'you never get a second chance to make a first impression'. A disproportionate amount of employee turnover happens in the first 90 days.[3] This is costly and time consuming.

It's all too easy to succumb to the temptation of getting the new hire into their new role as quickly as possible, with hiring managers screaming for resource today. But it's critical to take the time to get the employee comfortable and confident and up to speed with the organization and its culture. Otherwise, all those great promises you made could be seen as false ones and your carefully crafted EVP flies out the window.

Even large, outwardly successful organizations struggle with this issue. But there is a false economy in getting people 'in place' before they are truly prepared to take on their role – it's easy to lose one, two or even six months of productivity as people find their feet. If you make the right hires, and onboard them in a planned, managed and coherent way over those critical first 90 days, you won't have to go back to square one.

Induction and onboarding can begin before the person joins. Leading organizations (such as The Coca-Cola Company in Europe) provide a new starters' intranet which helps keep the new hire warm and begins the process of induction in the interim period before they join. This allows them to connect with their new team, read things like the Code of Conduct, even complete some administrative paperwork. It's also important to ensure that the onboarding and induction isn't just about the routine (and important) things like health and safety, environment, processes and forms – get people connected to the culture and the brand. Do it in an interactive and engaging manner and people will feel they are part of the organization faster. Days invested at this front end pay dividends later.

5 Work experience

The day-to-day work experience should also deliver on your EVP. Traditionally, this is where people talk about 'employee engagement' – but engagement is really the entire experience, not just this segment of it.

It's critical to appreciate that no single function or entity owns employee engagement – just as with your customers, no single function owns that relationship. The best engagement efforts and practices involve a joined-up approach that is consciously managed across the business and shared explicitly by the key functions – human resources, internal communications, organizational development, finance, information technology, marketing, corporate communications, change management, leadership and management.

If one part of the organization, explicitly or implicitly, is seen to 'own' employee engagement in anything more than a coordinating manner, risks emerge:

- Efforts will tend to come from a biased functional perspective, so will not be fully integrated and will address only certain elements of the employee engagement picture.

- Efforts will have less buy-in and commitment from other functions and areas of the organization.

- Efforts will have less impact since they will apply fewer resources deployed from one functional budget.

- Efforts will be inefficient and probably duplicative as different stakeholders pursue different ideas with different approaches and no shared agenda.

Chapter 8 will discuss a recommended approach to ensuring that these risks are mitigated – largely through the creation of a single set of ideas to which the entire organization aligns, from the leadership down to every employee.

But even if you don't take that approach, the critical success factor is aligning to one key concept or set of ideas. Among these are vision, values, mission, strategy, customer-centricity, your people agenda, corporate responsibility, and many others. For obvious reasons, your brand and positioning can form a very powerful central organizing principle. But whatever principle you choose, ensure that everything else aligns to it in a sensible and carefully mapped out way.

Many practitioners will have a deep belief in the supremacy of one or more of these potential central organizing principles. Naturally, these will be biased towards the perspective from which they view things. It's probable that HR will want to see the centre of gravity around the human capital and people agenda, while marketing will come at things from a customer proposition perspective, and so on.

Talent management and career development

Part of the experience will involve communication and engagement with HR-related issues, from risk management organizational development, career planning, performance assessment, training, learning and development, reward and recognition, and related topics. This is all important content and critical to a high-performance organization. But it is important that these align to the central organizing principle. All too often, separate ideas or agendas (and even internal sub brands) are introduced that appeal to the desire for something differentiating and impactful from the functional perspective, but can prove confusing to the employee and adding to the 'noise' in the organization.

If it's a truism that your people are your brand, then it follows that HR communications – in design, tone, messaging and content – should exude and express your brand (and the EVP element that is a big part of it) to this audience. Better still, your operational practices and processes should also reflect the brand and the EVP. It's no good espousing 'simplicity' as a corporate value or brand attribute and then deploying a career development and competency framework that requires an advanced diploma in HR to unwind.

Increasingly, organizations that perform well in this space are moving their talent management agenda into a more strategic space. While there are ample resources available online and elsewhere, leading practice seems to be taking a longer-term approach to the resourcing pipeline.

What this means is that organizations are identifying where they want and need to grow the business in the coming three to five years, are identifying the talent they will need to achieve this, and then working back to identify a mix of the talent they already have (and can develop) and the talent they do not have (and need to attract) to create a far more long-term, managed strategy. This approach includes creating clear career paths and development stages, mapping so-called 'destination roles' and how employees can target and achieve these, and generally seeking to take a more quantifiable and managed approach to the whole process.

In so doing, an organization can inherently take the opportunity to ensure its entire talent attraction, management and development process is hard-wired to its brand and business strategy. Although the task itself is complex, alignment to the brand can and should provide a clear filter to clarification and simplification.

Employee brand engagement

Another key engagement requirement is for employees to understand and be able to deliver on the brand promise. Imagine the scenario: You've invested in brand building and raised awareness and consideration. Sales and marketing are generating numerous qualified leads. Leaders and line managers have all lined up to a clear and compelling strategy. The product and service are superb at a price that generates healthy margin. The retail and office environments are oozing your core purpose with confidence and clarity. HR has managed to fill the roles you need to grow and perform.

And then, your customers encounter your employees. Whether they are on the proverbial shop floor, in a call centre, in sales, working in the back office, providing advice, on the sideline at a sports event, or licking envelopes: does every one of them understand your brand, what it stands for, where it is going, and what their role is in delivering it?

This is employee brand engagement. Some call it 'living the brand'. It's making sure that everyone in the organization, particularly those with the most critical contact with the people who pay the bills (the customer), are DOING what the brand is SAYING. So leaders and managers are walking the talk. Line managers understand the brand and are equipped with the tools and confidence to make sure their teams do, too. Employees are able to make the right kinds of decisions and know what to do in their day-to-day work to make it happen.

This doesn't mean you need to create an army of 'brand-washed' clones – that would defeat the purpose of the many benefits your brand and culture derives from a diverse and inclusive workforce. But on the other hand, if you are smart about the way you have crafted your brand and your EVP, and the way your functions align to your brand purpose, then you are halfway there. You will have attracted the right talent from a diverse range of backgrounds who share your brand's vision. You will continue to inspire, develop, retain and grow the people you have. When they leave, they will be vocal advocates for your organization.

But your efforts must be planned, managed and sustained across functions and operations to achieve this. You must invest in engagement efforts, on an ongoing basis, to maintain it.

Change communications

Even the way you manage change is critical. Change, often large, rapid and unexpected, is a given in today's dynamic marketplaces. Given that organizations and their ecosystems are complex, it can be virtually impossible to predict, let along manage, how a change in one part of the system will affect another part of the system.

How you manage and engage people in this change is also part of delivering the employee experience aligned to your brand. Whether the change is coming from inside or outside, you need to ensure you engage people in what it is, why it is happening, what its effects are likely to be, and what people should do as a result. Change programmes generally fail because of lack of buy-in and poor communication. So here are some tips any brand and talent management thinker should take when communicating and engaging people in change:

- Involve the people affected by the change in helping to plan how to manage it and communicate about it. The best way to take people with you is to give them a role in shaping the response to change.

- Understand how change unfolds. A web search on 'the change curve' should provide sufficient insight into the emotional states people go through when confronted with change – from raised emotions and expectations to the 'valley of despair' before the proverbial light at the end of the tunnel. People also experience emotional phases – shock, anger, denial, then acceptance or any one of a number of models. Forewarned is forearmed; use this knowledge to shape your engagement approach – and keep it on brand.

- Be honest. If you don't know, say you don't know. If you are still working on solutions, say so. And communicate about it, so people won't fill in their own versions of the truth to improve upon your silence.

- Plan. These are of limited use but the act of planning is priceless. Plan scenarios, mitigate risk. Nothing will go precisely to any plan but at least you will have a direction of travel – and something, ideally, aligned to your central organizing principle if you are true to it.

Departure experience

Usually, and increasingly given the demographics of the workforce and increasing globalization, people meet the challenges of their role and begin to think about moving up, moving over or moving out. They seek to get what they need from the employment experience by seeking something different.

Sometimes, this means you can provide something different, by having in place career development plans, interesting career path opportunities, development opportunities such as mobility – so you can often provide a new challenge within your organization. Other times, whether the reasons are within your control or not, the person will move on to another challenge outside your organization. Even if the person is exiting your organization for less than ideal reasons, it is still a good idea to manage the exit experience as part of delivering on your overall EVP. You want as many people as possible who leave your organization to remain an advocate for it.

Consider an organization with 20 per cent employee turnover. This means that every five years you are creating a population of alumni that is as large as your company. Managing the alumni experience is an increasingly important part of the overall brand and talent management mix – and it has never been easier, thanks to social media technologies. Why is this so critical to your brand?

- People who leave may want to come back someday – so-called 'boomerangs'.
- People who leave may recommend your organization as a service provider to others.
- People who leave may become clients, suppliers or partners.
- If you treat them poorly when they leave, they will become brand detractors. This will have a negative influence on your reputation and your net promoter score. The positives gained from social media and word of mouth are very easily converted into negatives.

The building blocks of employee communications

No book on employee communications would be complete without reference to what I call the 'three Ms': Measurement, Messages and Media. While the earlier parts of this chapter cover some of the theoretical foundations of a robust approach to employee communication and engagement, the building blocks are making sure you are getting the right information to – and from – people at the right time, in the right way, and in doing so achieving the desired outcomes for everyone involved (your people, customers and stakeholders).

Once again, this chapter provides only an overview of this – as there are many specialist publications in print and online that go into far greater detail about these important and essential elements of employee communications. However, it is important to cover some of the basics.

Before we get started...

A fundamental point around the practice of employee communications and engagement: the world of top-down, one size fits all is no longer appropriate given the dynamics we've reviewed in this book. Nor is what many traditionally call 'two-way' communications – which is actually still top-down, one-way communications that happens to have a feedback loop or measurement mechanisms attached to it. That's still not really a two-way conversation any more than my making statements to you and then asking if you understand or agree with the statements – without really allowing for a meaningful response.

Effective employee communication and engagement should be based on not just understanding your audience, but engaging with them and co-creating the right communication environment with them. They will usually be able to tell you what works and what doesn't – and since different people have different preferences, you will no doubt need to manage a number of different methods to hold the conversation.

Situational leadership

Just the same, don't forget the 'situational leadership' model.[4] The basis of situational leadership theory is that there is no single 'best' style of leadership. Effective leadership is about the best approach to deal with the specific context and the task at hand. Successful leaders are those that adapt their leadership and communication style to the situation and who they are working with at any given moment – 'the capacity to set high but attainable goals, willingness and ability to take responsibility for the task, and relevant education and/or experience of an individual or a group for the task'. The age of the 'one style, my way or the highway' leader may be fading. In other words, sometimes 'command and control, top-down, directive communication' is fully appropriate, just as sometimes an open and honest, transparent dialogue could suit the requirements of the situation.

This is where many practitioners and providers come apart – they feel compelled to adhere to a particular mindset or model based on a belief in the supremacy of a particular approach. For example: the manager is always the most appropriate source of information; social intranets are the panacea for internal communications; face to face is the best approach in all circumstances; print media is old fashioned in the digital age. You will encounter many of these – none of them is actually true (or false, for that matter – it all depends).

In the real world, great communication is not just about some theory about what good communication is – it is firmly rooted in the reality of the moment, the dynamics of the situation, the task at hand and the people involved. It's for this reason that an over-reliance on so-called 'best practices' that worked elsewhere can lead to sub-optimal results. 'Best practice' is not a substitute for thinking, or for ideas.

Diversity

This is probably as good a place as any to cover the topic of diversity. If situational leadership means that leaders and communicators should be flexible and adapt their approach and style to the situation and people at hand, the modern tenets of true 'diversity and inclusiveness' dictate that having a robust and diverse cross-section of perspectives and background in the first place gets you off to a great start. There are numerous academic studies that demonstrate the importance of diversity in order to drive higher performance and innovation within organizations.

It's important to realize that 'diversity' has often been misinterpreted – so here is a good explanation from The Stanford Graduate School of Business Diversity and Work Group Performance faculty:

> People tend to think of diversity as simply demographic, a matter of color, gender, or age. However, groups can be disparate in many ways.
>
> Diversity is also based on informational differences, reflecting a person's education and experience, as well as on values or goals that can influence what one perceives to be the mission of something as small as a single meeting or as large as a whole company.
>
> Diversity among employees can create better performance when it comes to out-of-the-ordinary creative tasks such as product development or cracking new markets, and managers have been trying to increase diversity to achieve the benefits of innovation and fresh ideas.

Diversity and performance studies have been conducted at a range of institutions ranging from Stanford to Rutgers University to Wharton Business School at the University of Pennsylvania, Harvard Business School and MIT's Sloan School of Management, to name just a few. The basic truth: *Teams comprised of people from a variety of backgrounds typically outperform those that are homogeneous – but only if they are managed well.*

Some of the most striking divergences can be seen in the areas of problem-solving, conflict resolution, and creativity. In these three crucial skill sets, diverse groups have been shown consistently to outperform their homogeneous counterparts.[5]

One particular US study[6] presents data relating to talent diversity and brand. Directly quoting:

- Diversity increases sales and profit but also notes a relationship between diversity and the number of customers.
  - Companies reporting the highest levels of racial diversity brought in nearly 15 times more sales revenue on average than those with the lowest levels of racial diversity.
  - Gender diversity accounted for a difference of $599.1 million in average sales revenue: organizations with the lowest rates of gender diversity had average sales revenues of $45.2 million, compared with averages of $644.3 million for businesses with the most gender diversity.
- Diversity directly pays off in sales and especially expanding the customer base:
  - For every percentage increase in the rate of racial or gender diversity up to the rate represented in the relevant population, there was an increase in sales revenues of approximately 9 per cent and 3 per cent, respectively.
  - The more diverse the company the larger the customer base. Gender diversity was even more critical than racial diversity, with companies that were the most gender diverse having an average of 15,000 more customers than the least diverse.
- Analysis of National Organizations Survey data for 506 US-based businesses also found that diversity levels and profits relative to peer companies rose in tandem.

However, there is a big caveat: the benefits of diversity require a unique kind of enlightened management in order to deliver on the promise. According to a *Harvard Business Review*[7] article (among others):

> Diverse teams are prone to dysfunction because the very differences that feed creativity and high performance can also create communication barriers. Conventional team-building activities are unreliable for such groups, because their one-size-fits-all approach to building cohesion fails to recognize team members' idiosyncratic strengths and weaknesses and how they can be combined to make the whole greater than the sum of its parts.

In other words, you can't just put a bunch of diverse people together and expect the job to be done. Reaping the benefits of high-performance teaming from a diverse group requires a specific set of leadership, cultural and management attributes.

> The interview with Beth Brooke of EY in Chapter 16 provides some pragmatic insight into the relationships among brand, talent and diversity from one of the world's leading advocates in this area – and the attributes of the kind of leader who can make the most of diverse talent.

Messages

If you can't explain it to a six-year-old, you don't understand it yourself.

(Albert Einstein)

You need to be clear what you are trying to say before you say it, of course. But this is easier said than done, because in most organizations today an employee is being bombarded by simultaneous messages from a range of communicators – internally and externally, near and far. Most of the senders are clear on what they want to say. But all too often the resulting cacophony is just noise. It makes it very difficult for the receiver to select which is the most important, and where to focus their attention.

Information overload and information fatigue syndrome (IFS)[8] are very real phenomena with big business impact. A Reuters study found that due to IFS:

- 38 per cent of managers surveyed waste 'substantial' amounts of time just looking for information;
- 43 per cent of respondents thought that decisions were delayed and otherwise adversely affected by 'analysis paralysis' or the existence of too much information;
- 47 per cent of respondents said that information collection distracts them from their main responsibilities – they find it difficult to develop strategies for dealing with the information they retrieve;
- 42 per cent attributed ill-health to this stress;

- 61 per cent said that they have to cancel social activities as a result of information overload;
- 60 per cent said that they are frequently too tired for leisure activities.

Our Huawei example from Chapter 3 is a good one. Without even delivering any content, it is possible to have created a framework of 20 or more categories for an employee to be simultaneously contemplating – before we have even spoken about the job at hand or the information we are trying to share.

While every organization will have a great deal of day-to-day, business-as-usual (BAU) information it needs to share, one way to help enhance communication efforts is to make sure that wherever and whenever possible, your messages are locked (or at least loosely attached) to an overarching framework. If you do this, you will (just as with your external brand engagement efforts) create a 'red thread' that should reduce the amount of 'optionality' in your communications and make it easier for both those creating messages and those receiving them to see what is important.

CLC[9] research supports this. Their data show that the top five drivers of engagement include:

1 connection between work and organizational strategy;
2 importance of job to organizational success;
3 understanding of how to complete work projects;
4 internal communication;
5 strong commitment to diversity.

The pragmatic application of this is clear: even for day-to-day BAU communication it is essential to make connections to organizational strategy and success. This means that even standalone functionally driven communications should not deviate from the more strategic elements of an organization's vision and mission. It also means that one should avoid creating a range of 'branded' internal initiatives to help differentiate and help these initiatives cut through the organizational noise – because all they will be doing is creating more of it.

In essence, once you have picked a peg to hang your hat on you need to stick with it, relentlessly. The creation of simple messaging frameworks is a good way to do this. In many cases there is an overarching strategic version of this framework or 'message house', with more detailed versions for key audiences and markets – but all align to the overarching messages (Figure 7.2).

FIGURE 7.2 A messaging framework

OVERARCHING MESSAGE		
KEY MESSAGE 1	**KEY MESSAGE 2**	**KEY MESSAGE 3**
• Proof point 1 • Proof point 2 • Proof point 3	• Proof point 1 • Proof point 2 • Proof point 3	• Proof point 1 • Proof point 2 • Proof point 3

These frameworks should include three main messages ideally – although in some exceptional cases it might be possible to have four or – at the absolute maximum – five. The 'rule of three' has been studied by everything from psychology to religion to comedy to speeches to screenplays and used as a powerful and simple way to enhance the effectiveness of communication.

Consider the following from Listly,[10] a blog about, well, lists and a small sample of 'rule of three' examples:

Religion

- Father, Son, and Holy Spirit
- Heaven, hell, and purgatory
- Three Wise Men
- ... with their gold, frankincense, and myrrh
- Faith, Hope and Charity

Repetition

- 'This is not the end. It is not even the beginning of the end. But it is, perhaps, the end of the beginning' (Sir Winston Churchill)
- 'The rule is: jam tomorrow, and jam yesterday, but never jam today' (Lewis Carroll, *Through the Looking Glass*)
- 'Our priorities are Education, Education, Education' (Tony Blair)
- 'Location, Location, Location' (real estate)
- 'Three Strikes You're out!' (baseball – and the US government)

- 'Government of the people, by the people, for the people'
  (the Gettysburg Address)

Trios

- 'Veni, Vidi, Vici' (I came, I saw, I conquered) (Julius Caesar)
- 'Friends, Romans, Countrymen lend me your ears'
  (William Shakespeare)
- 'A Mars® a day helps you work, rest and play' (advertising slogan)
- 'Stop, look and listen' (public safety announcement)
- 'Rock, Paper, Scissors' (game)
- 'Blood, sweat and tears' (Winston Churchill)
- 'The good, the bad and the ugly' (Clint Eastwood)
- 'It's as easy as one, two, three' (common English expression).

The human mind is very adept at remembering sets of three (with one adage being to use three messages – plus or minus two, giving you a maximum range of one to five messages).

Within each framework is one key, overarching message and three supporting messages. Each supporting message should then be supported by evidence, proof points and reasons to believe – since, of course, you will have to be able to support your messages with facts.

This three-message approach often encounters resistance in organizations, regardless of their size and complexity. However, as a business management and communication discipline, the act of enforcing this focus and prioritization is an incredibly potent exercise. It is also something that can and should be done in consultation and collaboration – with leaders and with employees. There is at least one example of a large multinational recreating its values using a global three-day online and face-to-face event to engage the entire organization in crafting and agreeing its three values.

When done well, virtually any strategy communication, HR programme, marketing campaign, change management exercise, IT implementation, vision or values campaign can be mapped back to a solid three-message framework. Anything that doesn't map back instantly stands out as extraneous – questioning whether you should be saying it at all.

The interview with Michael Sneed, Global Head of Corporate Affairs for Johnson & Johnson, provides some powerful insights and perspective on this very issue in Chapter 20.

Media

The other guys think the purpose of communication is to get information.
We think the purpose of information is to foster communication.

(Mark Zuckerberg, founder & CEO of Facebook)

Once you know what you want to say, you then need to find the best time and place to talk with your audience about it. What is often forgotten is: What is the meaning and value of what you are saying to your audience? How does it affect them? What do you expect them to think, feel, or do as a result? Organizational communications frequently generate information without taking this into account. This can also raise a lot of challenges and complexity, because there are generally a number of different channels available across an organization, and, as mentioned earlier, different people have different preferences in terms of how they consume information and contribute to the conversation about it.

There are plenty of books and articles about the Dos and Don'ts of channels – from e-mail to intranets to social media to newsletters to town hall meetings to cascades to videos to interactive exercises and a lot more. I do not propose to go into them all here.

In general, stick to three principles:

1 Select a media channel or approach because it is one that your audience trusts, uses and resonates with – not because you can or because it exists or is being hyped at a given moment.

2 Use more than one appropriate channel with any important communication – and use it again. Repetition is the mother of knowledge; sometimes you need to say things three times before people take it aboard.

3 When in doubt, ask. You will often be surprised by the result.

Measurement

If we can't identify a decision that could be affected by a proposed measurement and how it could change those decisions, then the measurement simply has no value.

(Douglas W Hubbard)[11]

Measurement is important: How do you demonstrate the value and the effect of your communication efforts? How do you adjust your approach to get the most out of it? We need to know whether what we are doing is making any difference, because if it isn't – we need to try a different approach.

Quantitative approaches

Once again, there are numerous approaches to deciding what to measure, why to measure it, how to measure it, when to measure it and what to do with the results. An entire industry of employee opinion and engagement surveys has emerged from the service profit chain article of 1994; you would be hard-pressed to find an organization that does not undertake a large-scale measurement activity of one kind or another.

It's often said that 'What gets measured gets managed', and therein lies the most significant challenge with using quantitative engagement surveys. Despite great efforts, often the numbers these studies generate can be very difficult to use to drive action. What frequently happens is that the focus shifts from effective communication and engagement efforts to moving some numbers up the dial in the report to the executive team. This might well be true for many facets of management information and reporting, but there is a challenge when it comes to employee engagement data.

With financial figures, it is easy to use mathematical analysis to create decision models, because there are tangible things called dollars (or pounds, yen, whatever) that can be precisely counted. They're real. In social science, which relies on the science of statistics and probabilities, a value is being *assigned* to something. It is real, but the assigned value is completely hypothetical. It is not being measured in the same way as the dollars or yen sitting in an account or generated as a result of a sale. Similarly, on any given day (indeed at different times on the same day), a human being might give very different answers to the same question on a survey.

Statistics is simply the science of whether the results obtained in a particular survey would be replicated if the survey were conducted many times over. That is all statistical significance is – if I ran the study again, $x\%$ of the time the results would be within $y\%$ of the numbers we observed. As a result:

> Statistical tests are supposed to guide scientists in judging whether an experimental result reflects some real effect or is simply a random fluke... even when performed correctly, statistical tests are widely misunderstood and frequently misinterpreted. It's science's dirty little secret: the widespread use of statistical science is more like a crapshoot.[12]

A second risk is the assumption that one organization's data can be benchmarked against an aggregate of data from similar (and, all too often, different) organizations. While this can provide an interesting 'finger in the air' in terms of how well one's own organization is doing, it might not be the most appropriate comparison metric to be using to drive one's own, unique organization and how it engages with its ecosystem. It is a data point to consider, not a target to hit.

A third risk is that sometimes employee survey data are used spuriously. For example, I participated in a debate where a leading employee survey practitioner made the blanket statement that social media should *never* be used to make a significant organizational announcement. My response was that surely, in a given situation, at a given time, with a given organization, on a given topic, it could indeed be appropriate – if, for example, that organization enjoyed strong adoption of social communications and had experienced success, or if that was the most effective way to get the message across in those circumstances. The response was unequivocal: the data indicated that social media was a preferred source of information for fewer than 10 per cent of the data set. And the data said that employees indicated that 'other employees' were either their first or second most-preferred source in fewer than 10 per cent of all cases. Therefore, as night follows day, you should not use social media for a major organizational announcement.

In other words: in hundreds of employee surveys with other companies, I asked people to rank-order their preferred source of communication (for example: senior leader, manager, intranet, newsletter, social media, other employees). I then make all my channel decisions based on that data – completely out of context.

I find that kind of logic baffling, and the exact opposite way to how survey data should be used, and why I have such a healthy scepticism for the way people sometimes try to use data from employee surveys. They are a set of numbers (some of which may be statistically significant – but still, see above) that should *inform* your decisions, not *mandate* them.

This is not intended as an attack on the use of quantitative employee surveys. They have their place as one data point in the bigger picture. Instead, it is a caution that, compared to the disproportionate level of investment that organizations tend to make in such studies, it could be argued that a more balanced and multifaceted approach to gauging the effectiveness of communications and engagement efforts should be considered.

For example, 'pulse surveys' – shorter, sharper and more frequent studies – is one way of smoothing the risk in larger-scale studies. They can also be used to address specific issues in specific populations at specific times, rather than the more onerous 'all-employees survey'.

Qualitative approaches

Qualitative approaches – such as interviews, focus groups, even anthropo-logical 'participant observation' approaches where employees are observed in their day-to-day jobs – can provide deeply valuable and insightful data. While these data's validity is sometimes challenged as lacking the 'statistical rigour' and representative sample of the more quantitative study, it should not be excluded wholly on that basis. After all, even 'experts in the math of probability and statistics are well aware of these problems, and have for decades expressed concern about them'.[13]

Qualitative research often allows a depth and breadth of detail that quantitative research cannot emulate. It allows exploration of topics that might have been identified, and therefore not even included within the quan-titative study at all. It often can generate the most insightful and 'human' expressions of issues, challenges and opportunities in an organization or its stakeholders.

In summary, when it comes to measurement, just as with media and channels: use a combination of approaches that work in concert to achieve your objectives. Never rely on just one way of doing things. And make sure that whatever measures you are using help you make better decisions – or you shouldn't be using them.

Summary

We have covered the basics around branding and brand management. And we have covered the basics around talent engagement and communica-tion and their linkages to some of the disciplines of talent management.

The discussion so far should provide you with enough general informa-tion to be able to address the increasingly interrelated challenges of brand management and talent management in the way that most organizations do today: a mix of best practices, and cross-functional collaboration to try to align the organization around a core set of ideas for both its internal and external stakeholders.

Are you ready?

Some think there must be a better way to align brand management and talent management from a communication and engagement perspective, in such a way that both are hardwired into not only what an organization says, but also what it does.

The next chapter introduces this more integrated approach. It has been pioneered by creative strategy consultancy BrandPie.

By way of disclosure, I am a partner at BrandPie, and this approach was developed by me and the other partners over the course of several assignments with a range of organizations ranging from multinational professional services firms with more than 150,000 employees around the world, to a global pharmaceutical company, to a North American technology company and others. We believe it is a powerful model that is deceptively simple – and therein lies its strength.

Notes

1 Content in this chapter has been adapted from my book *The Talent Journey: The 55-minute guide to employee communication*. Used with permission.

2 LinkedIn (2010) Why Your Employer Brand Matters

3 Chartered Institute of Personnel Development (CIPD) (2012) Employee Turnover and Retention Factsheet, July

4 Hersey, P and Blanchard, K H (1972) *Management of Organizational Behavior: Utilizing human resources*, 2nd edn, Prentice Hall, Englewood Cliffs, NJ

5 Page, Scott E (2007) *The Difference: How the power of diversity creates better groups, firms, schools, and societies,* Princeton University Press, Princeton, NJ

6 American Sociological Association (2009) Workplace diversity pays: research links diversity with increased sales revenue and profits, more customers, *American Sociological Review*, April

7 Polzer, J *et al* (2008) Making diverse teams click, *Harvard Business Review*, July

8 Lewis, D (1996) in *Dying For Information? A report on the effects of information overload in the UK and worldwide*, Reuters

9 Corporate Leadership Council (2004) *Driving Performance and Retention through Employee Engagement*, The Conference Board

10 http://blog.list.ly [accessed 11 October 2013]

11 Hubbard, D (2007) *How to Measure Anything: Finding the value of 'intangibles' in business*, John Wiley & Sons, Chichester

12 Siegfried, T (2010) Odds are, it's wrong: science fails to face the shortcomings of statistics, *Science News*, March

13 Siegfried, T (2010)

PART THREE
Brand and talent

A better way

If the rate of change on the outside exceeds the rate of change on the inside, the end is near.

(JACK WELCH)

Making the connection

The first part of this book talks a lot about the general state of play regarding brand and reputation management. The second part delves into talent attraction, engagement and management. In both parts, a clear case has been established that the two are inextricably linked and have a reciprocal effect on organizational performance.

If the connection and overlap between the worlds of brand management and talent management are so obvious, why then does it appear to be so difficult to wring efficiencies and improved performance from this overlap? As you will have gathered from the beginning of this book, a great deal of the challenge comes from the very way organizations are put together. The separation of responsibilities by audience and by task, appropriate for another era, is appearing to be less useful, agile and effective in the new age.

It would, on the other hand, be foolish to assert that functional specialist expertise is not required – rather, the challenge lies around *how* that functional specialism and expertise is integrated and applied in concert with other functions. Most organizations have not really changed their operational models to deal with the whirling dynamics of their external environment. Many, perhaps like the Huawei example, have found themselves in what might be an uncomfortable place when it comes down to what messages the organization should be focusing on. For employees, they might be forgiven for scratching their heads and wondering which thing they should be worried about – or, more likely, just 'disengage' and get on with making widgets.

> If you want to gather some interesting perspectives about this, and want a good way to whet your appetite for the rest of this chapter, you could do worse than to read the interview in Chapter 17 with Dave Coplin, Chief Envisioning Officer at Microsoft and author of *Business Reimagined*.

Add to this the confusion and competition among different models and ways of thinking about brand and talent, coming from the different worlds of marketing, human resources, business strategy, communications and elsewhere, and it is not surprising that there are challenges in getting any sort of alignment to happen.

Where to begin?

Step one

The first step is perhaps the hardest for those who have done the drill before, or more painfully those who advise them: Dispose of a lot of the terminology that has crept into the world of business strategy, brand and talent management.

With words we make our world. The basis of human communication is whether the meaning behind the word that I say matches the picture in your mind when you hear it.

So some words should be banned from the process entirely. We all need a clean sheet of paper. This will prove uncomfortable to many who have very specific and strong views about organizational strategy and development. Nonetheless, by changing the words we use we provide ourselves with a new and arguably level playing field on which to start the conversation.

What words should we ban – at least in this specific context?

- vision, vision statement;
- mission, mission statement;
- goals;
- objectives;
- brand values, attributes, etc;
- any combination of these words that is different in different parts of the organization;
- brand, employer brand.

Uncomfortable yet? While it might seem to be just a rhetorical device, setting aside these baggage-laden terms can prove to be very liberating. Particularly when working with senior management, shifting the lexicon allows for a mindshift and avoids debating different and deep-set views about specific terms and their application.

In a moment, we'll come back to the words the new model suggests. But first, we need to explore the rationale and thinking behind the model in the next step.

Step two

The second step is to stop separating branding and external communications and engagement from talent communications and engagement when it comes to their definition and alignment. They can and should be managed by functional experts – but ownership of the core ideas and expression must exist at the higher level to ensure alignment and focus.

This means that you have one brand and one core set of ideas. Each function or audience does not get its own version to play with. You co-create and agree one together, and you stick to it.

Remember the customer lifecycle and the employee lifecycle? What this model proposes is that they live side by side. They must be lined up side by side, or seen as two sides of the same sheet of paper (if that analogy works better for you), for your brand and talent management to work in an integrated way.

To do this requires you to think about your reputation as an organization and your reputation as an employer as two sides of the same coin. Both sides must draw their inspiration and expression from the same set of core component elements or they will not be aligned. This approach can be simply expressed using the model shown in Figure 8.1.[1]

On the one hand, at first glance this might not appear to be a radical concept or approach. Common sense, it is often said, can be uncommon. When most people see it, it seems quite obvious. This is part of its power and appeal.

On the other hand, the reality is that few organizations actually approach their brand management, talent management and communications in this manner. Brand, strategy, marketing, employer brands, talent acquisition, go-to-market programmes are, all too often, misaligned and marching to their own drum beat (often to the click of a functionally set metronome). While few would argue that engaging and aligning people to deliver the right customer experience is critical to success, the reality of the cut-and-thrust of day-to-day business and functional agendas can drive a wedge between efforts.

FIGURE 8.1   BrandPie's brand and talent model, copyright © 2012

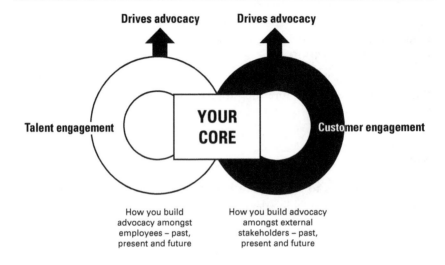

Some organizations have grasped this nettle and are demonstrating its power in terms of their operational structure and how they communicate where they are going, both internally and externally.

These include, among others:

- *IBM*. Its 'Smarter Planet' core infuses everything they do across 10 distinct data-driven disciplines.

- *Accenture*. 'High performance. Delivered.' is their unavoidable mantra.

- *EY*. 'Building a better working world' through 'Exceptional client service and high performance teaming' permeates not just communications but operations across 170,000 people globally.

- *Johnson & Johnson*. This Top 10 global pharmaceutical company's 'Credo' sits atop clear aspirations, strategy and growth drivers.

- *Mahindra*. One of India's powerhouse conglomerates has one overall 'House of Mahindra' framework that aligns 160,000 people across 18 wildly different industry sectors in 100 countries.

- *Interface* (the world's leader in sustainable, modular carpeting). Its entire business is driven, and its performance enhanced by, seeking to achieve what it calls 'Mission Zero' – zero waste and environmental impact.

What is interesting is that the shift to too many messages and ideas is something that has happened in the previous 15 years. Before this, there were many examples of organizations that had managed to focus and simplify who they were and what they stood for. It is likely that the combination of social, economic and, most importantly, technological change – and globalization – has caused organizations to lose sight of the required simplicity. They have instead been left to wallow in their own confused complexity as they are forced to react, on a quarter-by-quarter basis, to burning platforms and what they perceive to be more imminent and emergent challenges – each generating new messages and adding to the noise and confusion.

So what lies at the core?

The above model aligns the customer lifecycle (efforts to influence your reputation with external stakeholders so that you drive Awareness, Consideration, Preference and Advocacy) with the employee lifecycle (attract, recruit, engage, develop and export your talent).

So: what lies at the core? In the following chapters we will address each of these elements in a bit more detail. But this framework in brief includes (Figure 8.2):

1 *Purpose.* This is a crisp, clear, compelling, confident statement that answers the question, 'Why do you exist?' Why do you and your people get out of bed in the morning? Why would your market and the world be a poorer place if you simply ceased to exist? What do you generate beyond profit and what impact do your activities have on your people, your communities and the larger world?

2 *Ambition.* What have you set out to achieve? What is that mountain you have set out to climb? How will you measure or monitor your progress or success along the way? When will you know you have done it (will you ever?)

3 *Strategy.* What is your plan to get there? What activities is the business doing (and what activities is it not going to do), with whom, where and in what order to achieve your Ambition and fulfil your Purpose? How does each person make their contribution?

4 *Proposition.* Given all of this, within your competitive landscape, how will you express what makes you special and unique to your marketplace? What is your value proposition when it really comes down to service delivery or product performance? Is it relevant? Is it authentic? Is it different, and does that difference matter?

FIGURE 8.2   The P-A-S-P model

PURPOSE	AMBITION	STRATEGY	PROPOSITION
Why you exist	What you aim to achieve	Your plan to get there	How you best express it

Top line: A concise 5-word version	**Top line:** 3 (+/−2) goals – financial or otherwise	**Top line:** 3 (+/−2) activities operations align to	**Top line:** A concise 5–10-word version
Elevator pitch: A 100-word version	**Elevator pitch:** A 20–30-word version for each	**Elevator pitch:** A 30–100-word version for each	**Elevator pitch:** A 100-word version
Deep dive: As long as you and your audience find interesting and useful	**Deep dive:** As long as you and your audience find interesting and useful	**Deep dive:** As long as you and your audience find interesting and useful	**Deep dive:** As long as you and your audience find interesting and useful

What about values?

The model in its most simple form does not contain corporate or brand values. This is not intended to diminish the importance of values to and for an organization by any stretch of the imagination. Far from it: values deserve special treatment because, first, there are very different levels of passion and belief about how to create them and how to embed them; and second, there are often different perspectives on how much emphasis to place on them, either formally or informally, as a cultural decision-making and behavioural compass.

A lot has been (and will be) written about the creation, adoption and activation of corporate values. Tom Peters and Bob Waterman[2] and others have long advocated the importance of a strong, clear set of values that help define, shape and guide an organization and its behaviours – ranging from the talent it seeks to attract and retain to the business practices it employs and even the customers it chooses to work with. It is hard to disagree with the concept or the sentiment. Collins and Porras[3] similarly advocate the paramount nature of a strong and clear set of guiding values as essential to the company that eclipses its competitors.

On the other hand, there is a degree of scepticism that can be applied to corporate values when they are not genuinely embedded in an organization. A study by Edwin Giblin and Linda Amuso of California State University found that values have to be internalized by employees in organizations to be real, and according to their research, this seldom happens.[4] This therefore raises a challenge: If you choose claim values, but do not deliver on them, you will create a gap between what you say and what you do. And, as we have already discussed, this damages the value of your brand.

> *Values are basic, fundamental, enduring and meant to be acted upon. In contrast, slogans, platitudes and tag lines are ephemeral, transitory and relative. For example, if a company's prime goal is short-term profits for shareholders, how can it espouse a corporate value of 'people are our greatest asset'?*[5]

Giblin and Amuso argue that corporate values must be 'first-order values'. First-order values are human and universal values which can't be altered in an economic downturn or a momentary crisis. They must therefore be elevated above direct commercial and business-related concepts. But most importantly, they must be fully ingrained in an organization's culture and behaviours. Clearly this is influenced by, and influences, both brand and talent communications, processes and behaviours.

For this reason, whether your organization chooses to enshrine these behavioural and decision-making ideals as values or in other ways, it is up to the individual organization to debate and agree their place within this model.

The recommended approach is to take a decision about (1) whether you believe your values remain relevant and (2) where you believe they fit best into this model.

Regarding the first point, by their very nature corporate values should not be subject to change frequently (if ever). On the other hand, some organizations either need to generate, or wish to refresh, their values.

Second, if you want to accommodate the role of values in this model, you need to consider the best place for them. They can easily be accommodated with any of the sections of the model – aligned to your Purpose; achieved as part of your Ambition; a core behavioural element that drives your Strategy; or hardwired into your Proposition.

Personally, when I work with leadership teams to craft or refine values, I insist on two things. First, just as we ban certain words from the 'brand' lexicon, we ban 'motherhood and apple pie' words from the values debate and strive to focus on authentic, plain language, actionable sets of words – and, of course, limit them to three in total. Among the banned words – because too often they have become meaningless or clichéd through over- and mis-use – are: integrity, teamwork, collaboration, innovation. Trust me, there are better ways to say these things. Second, it must involve as many people from inside and outside the organization as is practicable.

So the complete model looks like this: a unified core which we call Purpose, Ambition, Strategy and Proposition (Figure 8.3). This is then used as the core set of principles which drive all relevant (and most must be) communication and operational efforts around both the 'customer' (external stakeholder) universe and the 'talent' (internal stakeholders including alumni) universe. Ultimately, this model can establish the core set of ideas that, when executed coherently across the organization and lived/breathed by everyone from the CEO to the newest recruit, can have a tremendous impact on ensuring clarity and alignment for both internal and external stakeholders.

FIGURE 8.3   The complete model

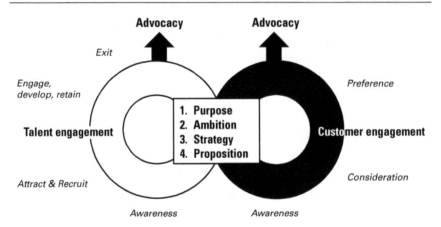

While we have focused on the customer and talent elements of the model for simplicity, keep in mind that your other stakeholders within your eco-system are also affected by, and affect, your reputation. Of course, there is an entire universe of stakeholders and third parties who are influencers and potential advocates. We've kept the model focused on customers and talent, while making reference to other stakeholders throughout, for the sake of simplicity.

But truly sustainable businesses don't just focus on their customers and their talent; they take a whole-systems view and ensure that their operations take into account their impact not only on their workplace and marketplace, but on their communities and the environment.

So if we are talking about truly integrated reputation management, the model (while still more or less elegantly symmetrical) is slightly more complex. Reputation management, of course, must cater for all stakeholders, and you must ensure you craft your P-A-S-P accordingly.

A fuller exploration of the model really looks like Figure 8.4.

FIGURE 8.4   Master P-A-S-P model

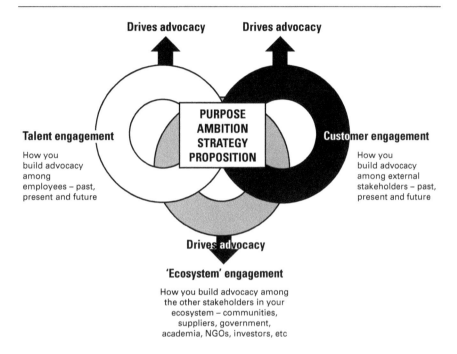

Step three

The next step is to perform some background analysis and to engage with your key stakeholders to populate this model. If you refer back to the range of stakeholders in Chapter 2, it's a good idea to get all of their views on board.

This is by its nature a comprehensive exercise, but it does not need to be onerous. All you are doing is asking some very open-ended, simple questions and reviewing how you have been talking about similar concepts like vision, mission and values in the past.

The five basic stages are:

1 *Audit yourself.* Audit your own processes and communications to sense-check levels of coherence and alignment. Are you consistent? Are you coherent? Are you credible? Are you clear? How different are your stakeholder messages – aligned to your core idea, or a bit all over the place?

2 *Engage stakeholders.* Have conversations with your stakeholders (for example, employees, customers, suppliers, partners, regulators) and ask questions about:

 – Why do you think we exist?

 – What makes who we are, what we do and how we do it valuable, different or special?

 – What do you value most about us as an organization?

 – What sorts of words or ideas do you associate with us?

 – Why would customers want to hire us or buy our products?

 – What is most important to you about the kind of service we provide or what we sell?

 – Why should people want to work here? Why do they stay? Why do they leave?

3 *Audit your competition* (in both the commercial and the talent marketplaces) to see what they say and do, and how they position themselves.

4 *Design possible solutions – and engage people again.* Explore different territories that you think you may wish to occupy in terms of your Purpose, Ambition and Proposition – and then, go back and test these in conversations with your stakeholders (internally and externally). Which do they think are the most accurate? The most distinctive? The most inspiring?

5 *Commit and execute.* Select your best set, and then assess what you will need to start doing, continue doing and stop doing in order to ensure ruthless consistency to your Purpose, Ambition, Strategy and Proposition across every facet of operations. You will need to establish business cases and in most cases commission change and transformation priorities, programmes, milestones and timelines (mapped from your Strategy to your Ambition and aligned to your Purpose and Proposition) to ensure you get there. But that is well covered in other books, too!

First stage – audit yourself

Performing a review/audit of an organization's existing messaging is required. You will need to look at a range of internal and external communications across your stakeholders and pick out the most high-profile ones to establish themes and patterns. Do you say more or less the same thing in relatively the same way to your different stakeholders, or do you have what appears to be a wide range of different messages and ways of expressing who you are and what you do to each of them? If you laid these communications out on a big table (and reviewed the various processes you put behind the communications – for example, in terms of sales, business development, recruiting, performance planning, reward and recognition, internal communications and so forth) – would they tell a cohesive story? Is there a central theme?

This first set of findings should provide you with a robust set of insights to consider as you craft your Purpose, Ambition, Strategy and Positioning.

Second stage – engage with stakeholders

Using a combination of approaches – ranging from one-to-one interviews to workshops/discussion groups – on and offline, you need to have some structured conversations with the people whom you believe have the greatest insights about, and the greatest influence upon, your reputation as an organization and as an employer.

Is what your leadership team believes aligned? Does it reflect the perceptions of the rest of the business – where, how and why or why not? Does that in turn match with what your external stakeholders – from clients to suppliers to regulators to journalists and analysts – think is important, true and unique about you? Are there hidden strengths you haven't made the most of, or things you thought were important that others frankly don't?

Third stage – audit your competition

Using similar criteria to those you used for your own organization, take a look at your competitors (both for market share and for talent – they can sometimes be very different). What are they saying and how are they saying it? How similar is it to what you say and do? How is it different? Are you all clustered in the same narrow area – or do some manage to stand out? How, and why?

Pick between six and eight. Look at 'the usual suspects' – but also select a couple of organizations that you and your team admire – what can you learn from them, what they do and how they do it?

Are you able to start forming some ideas around where stage one and two findings can help identify a space for you to carve out?

Fourth stage – design possible solutions, and engage people again

Use the insights you've gained from the first three stages and start to craft different variations on the model. So long as you have the audit trail to validate what direction you want to take, don't be afraid to be bold: you are exploring opportunities, and if you do not go into this stage with some ideas that are scary then you are not trying hard enough. Craft some different models and combinations of Purpose, Ambition, Strategy and Proposition. It is only through experimentation, exploration and debate that you will arrive at the right solution.

Then, you need to engage again with your stakeholders, this time presenting them with your findings and asking them to react to the various options you have created. Provide some relatively objective criteria for them to use (Relevant, Authentic and Differentiating is not a bad set to start with).

Fifth stage – commit and execute

Once you have tested your ideas and engaged with your stakeholders, you should be in a position to narrow it down to one or two options, fine-tune them and then make the big decision to commit to one. This commitment must be made and stuck to by the leadership team, and it must be clearly communicated to the rest of the organization.

The Strategy element is usually a challenging one. Depending on how different the new Purpose, Ambition, Strategy and Positioning are from the existing state, this can have implications for your brand, talent and operational processes and programmes. In many cases, this process can be the result of (or can put into action) a root-and-branch review of strategy. In most cases, the act of going through this process will have a positive impact on the focus and articulation of the strategy – it would be odd if it didn't!

The ultimate aim is to ensure that every part of the business is aware of, engaged in, and committed to aligning what they say and what they do to this overarching Purpose, Ambition, Strategy and Positioning. Little if any variation should be permitted as this defeats the purpose of going through the exercise.

In this way it is possible to create a core framework, created with and defined alongside cross-functional stakeholders as well as employees, customers and others, that drives ruthless consistency and clear focus in brand and talent management – one set of ideas and messages instead of different sets.

How is this different from other approaches?

In some ways, it could be argued that this is simply a rephrasing of a lot of standard approaches to establishing Vision, Mission, Values and Positioning, and that would be a fair challenge. Various approaches to setting corporate, brand and talent strategies are well documented and, for the most part, would not vary too much from this model.

On the other hand, cross-functional and cross-cultural and regional dynamics have created for many organizations a very convoluted and overly complex set of messages and ideas, inconsistently applied and with ample room for 'optionality' – often under the banner of 'localization'. It is my belief that the way to 'reset' this imbalance is to use the approach advocated here.

So while there are different models for addressing this, this approach:

- redefines some of the core terms with new ones that clearly are less battle-weary;
- keeps it simple – four core elements in plain language;
- allows for both inspirational higher-order content as well as commercially focused targets and business/operational content;
- aligns it to customer and talent marketplace messages in an integrated manner, rather than treating these as separate worlds.

In the following few pages, we'll dig a little deeper into Purpose, Ambition, Strategy and Proposition in turn.

Notes

1 BrandPie's brand and talent model, copyright © 2012

2 Peters, T and Waterman, R (1982) *In Search of Excellence: Lessons from America's best-run companies*, Harper & Row, New York. Often cited as one of the greatest business books of all time, by the authors' own admission the data were questionable

3 Collins, J and Porras, J (1994) *Built to Last: Successful habits of visionary companies*, Harper Business Essentials, New York; (2001) *Good To Great: Why some companies make the leap ... and others don't*, Harper Business, New York; and (1996) Building your company's vision, *Harvard Business Review*, September

4 Cited in Williams, R (2010) What do corporate values really mean?, *Psychology Today*, February

5 Williams, R (2010)

09 **Purpose**

> *Make your work to be in keeping with your purpose.*
>
> **(LEONARDO DA VINCI)**

A star to steer by

Much has been written about the idea of 'corporate vision/mission' and 'mission/vision statements'. For several decades they have run the gamut from the sublime to the frankly ridiculous – and sometimes hard to judge between the two. Like values, many feel them to be essential elements of the strategy and corporate leadership toolkit. And actually, they are. Such constructions can and should be created, and they should be useful tools for decision making and direction setting at the most fundamental and long-term level. They often start with the best, and the right, intentions.

The unfortunate truth is that, all too often, they become mired in committee wordsmithing, and inevitable (and, you guessed it, often functionally motivated) 'kitchen sink' mentality. Many of us will have experienced the 'tweaking' that turns a sharp 10-word vision into an interminable 50-word piece of corporate b.s.

This is a shame, because there is ample evidence that organizations that manage to establish and pursue a Purpose higher than the simple accumulation of profit for their shareholders actually outperform those who don't. It is for this reason that executive teams assemble to go through the ritual in the first place. Moreover, when executed with ruthless consistency, these statements can become a powerful tool that provides serious backbone that can help hold together and drive the entire organization: from brand to talent and beyond, through thick and thin.

The four-box model proposed in this book (Figure 9.1) seeks to streamline and accommodate this process by making 'space' for some of the frequently competing elements to occupy outside of the traditional vision and mission definitions. Each of the four boxes can accommodate some of the elements often muddled together in mission, vision, value, strategy and brand models. Some guidance is given relating to the word count – these are targets to aim for, but every organization must decide for itself how much it wants to include. Less is definitely more.

FIGURE 9.1 The P-A-S-P model

PURPOSE	**AMBITION**	**STRATEGY**	**PROPOSITION**
Why you exist	What you aim to achieve	Your plan to get there	How you best express it
Top line: A concise 5-word version	**Top line:** 3 (+/–2) goals – financial or otherwise	**Top line:** 3 (+/–2) activities operations align to	**Top line:** A concise 5–10-word version
Elevator pitch: A 100-word version	**Elevator pitch:** A 20–30-word version for each	**Elevator pitch:** A 30–100-word version for each	**Elevator pitch:** A 100-word version
Deep dive: As long as you and your audience find interesting and useful	**Deep dive:** As long as you and your audience find interesting and useful	**Deep dive:** As long as you and your audience find interesting and useful	**Deep dive:** As long as you and your audience find interesting and useful

Getting to a Purpose

The first step is understanding the definition of Purpose, as defined in the previous chapter. It's pretty simple: Why do you exist as an organization? What difference do you make for your stakeholders? Why would the world be a poorer place if you disappeared tomorrow?

A Purpose can be as grand and high level or as pragmatic and granular as you like. The most important point is that it is true, and that it is within the gift of your company to claim (or to play a role in contributing to). It's important not to drift into areas where an organization's workplace and marketplace activities don't have a material impact.

A Purpose should be short and sharp in its most concise incarnation – five words is a good goal. Of course, you can explain it in greater detail for the second and additional layers of information.

Is your Purpose your slogan or tagline?

The simple answer is: it depends. Some organizations may choose to use their Purpose as the primary driver of their corporate-level strategy and marketplace communication at the highest level. Others may use it less visibly, for example in internal communications, in their annual reporting, and as a banner for their corporate responsibility activities.

Given the building evidence around Purpose-driven brands, it is worth considering using your Purpose as your brand positioning.[1]

Is this a brand model then?

Organizations that adhere to this model will typically create brand and identity guidelines which, of course, align to, reflect and help bring this model to life through communications. I'd generally advise against creating a new raft of terms (brand values, attributes etc) since that can add to the noise you were just trying to simplify through this model. Nonetheless, so long as it is for use within the context of guidelines and guidance documents, particularly relating to tone of voice, you may wish to provide such additional detail. But do this sparingly.

What is a Purpose-driven brand?

A Purpose-driven brand is one where the organization has consciously placed its 'Why' front and centre – in how it communicates, but more importantly, in how it actually behaves in its business conduct. It drives what it will and will not do. It defines what services it provides, what products it sells, what people it hires, promotes and rewards – in other words, how it does business.

Some examples:

- Amazon: 'To enable freedom of choice.'
- IBM: 'Solutions for a smarter planet.'
- EY: 'Building a better working world.'
- SAP: 'Helping the world run better.'
- McKinsey & Company: 'World-changing client impact.'
- Unilever: 'Create a better future every day.'

- P&G: 'Purpose driven innovation.'
- The Coca-Cola System: 'To inspire moments of happiness.'
- Disney: Originally, 'To make people happy' (or in some places attributed as 'To create family magic'). They may possibly have fallen prey to the 'edit by committee' disease with their new version: 'To always deliver, with integrity, the most exceptional entertainment experiences for people of all ages.'

Many might see these sweeping statements as whitewash (or greenwash), over-claiming or jumping on the so-called 'sustainability' bandwagon. There is no doubt that many will attempt this. What makes the above companies different is that they are not simply saying it – they are organizing their business and operational models to explicitly and implicitly deliver on it.

A Purpose-driven brand since 1943: J&J's credo

Our Credo:
We believe our first responsibility is to the doctors, nurses and patients, to mothers and fathers and all others who use our products and services. In meeting their needs everything we do must be of high quality. We must constantly strive to reduce our costs in order to maintain reasonable prices. Customers' orders must be serviced promptly and accurately. Our suppliers and distributors must have an opportunity to make a fair profit.

We are responsible to our employees, the men and women who work with us throughout the world. Everyone must be considered as an individual. We must respect their dignity and recognize their merit. They must have a sense of security in their jobs. Compensation must be fair and adequate, and working conditions clean, orderly and safe. We must be mindful of ways to help our employees fulfil their family responsibilities. Employees must feel free to make suggestions and complaints. There must be equal opportunity for employment, development and advancement for those qualified. We must provide competent management, and their actions must be just and ethical.

We are responsible to the communities in which we live and work and to the world community as well. We must be good citizens – support good works and charities and bear our fair share of taxes. We must encourage civic improvements and better health and education. We must maintain in good order the property we are privileged to use, protecting the environment and natural resources.

Our final responsibility is to our stockholders. Business must make a sound profit. We must experiment with new ideas. Research must be carried on, innovative programs developed and mistakes paid for. New equipment must be purchased, new facilities provided and new products launched. Reserves must be created to provide for adverse times. When we operate according to these principles, the stockholders should realize a fair return.

This is Johnson & Johnson's credo values, drafted by former Chairman and member of the founding family Robert Wood Johnson. More information about Johnson & Johnson Services can be found on their website http://www.jnj.com/

Many see the pursuit of profit and a sense of higher purpose as an 'either profit or purpose' trade-off. But the leaders – philosophically and in financial performance – are discovering that it's actually a 'both profit and purpose' model. In fact, leaders see them as inseparable:

- 'This is not corporate social responsibility, it's not cause marketing, and it's not a strategy for philanthropy; it's a business strategy. Your philanthropy can come out of it, just like your R&D and HR come out of it. But once you choose your purpose – everything else should come out of that.' (Jim Stengel, former CMO, Procter & Gamble)[2]

- On Unilever's 'Sustainable Living Plan,' CEO Paul Polman says, 'This is not a new project to celebrate. This is a new business model to implement.'

- 'There is no more strategic issue for a company, or any organization, than its ultimate purpose.' (the late CEO of Interface, Ray Anderson)

- 'It's not an aspirational vision, but rather a practical way to address the kinds of problems that were seizing the world [...] and that still command our attention – from jobs and energy to the environment and the systemic problems of global finance.' (IBM CEO Sam Palmisano)

- 'We understand our obligation to look beyond our self-interest and engage with the world. We use our global reach and our relationships with clients, governments and not-for-profit organizations to create positive change.' (Mark Weinberger, CEO, EY)

- 'Companies that will lead in the 21st century define success more broadly than financial performance. They look at their impact on the world – socially, environmentally, and economically.' (Jim Hagemann Snabe, Co-CEO, SAP)

What evidence is there that Purpose-driven brands do any better than others?

There are numerous data sets, publications and studies you can discover on the topic of Purpose-driven brands. We'll cover a few here to establish the point:

- *87 per cent* – informed people who believe business should place 'equal weight' on society's interests and their own business goals. (Edelman Good Purpose Survey, 2012)

- *94 per cent* – CEOs who say that their company is 'increasingly held responsible not only for our own actions, but also for the actions of others in our value chain'. (Corporate Philanthropy CEO Conference 2010)

- *61 per cent* – of recent graduates that are likely to factor a company's commitment to sustainability into their decision if choosing between two jobs with the same location, responsibilities, pay and benefits (2011 Deloitte Volunteer IMPACT Survey)

- *62 per cent* – of the public across 20 countries 'say they trust corporations less now than they did a year ago'. (2009 Edelman Trust Barometer)

- *42* – the number of academic studies showing positive correlations between social enterprise and financial performance. (*Harvard Business Review*).

Havas Media Group published a global analytical framework[3] that looked at more than 700 brands in 23 countries and found some remarkable insights:

- Meaningful brands outperform the stock market by 120 per cent. Since 2004 the share prices of the top 25 companies on its Meaningful Brands Index (BMI) have increased faster than companies who are not seen as being meaningful by consumers.

- The Top 10 brands all scored above 50 per cent when asked if people would miss the brand if it disappeared tomorrow. The average across all brands was just 38 per cent.

- 70 per cent of people think that companies and brands should play a role in improving our quality of life and well-being.

- However, just 24 per cent of people agree that companies and brands are working hard at improving this.

- This is mirrored in Western Europe (29 per cent) and Eastern/Central Europe (31 per cent), Europe and the United States (28 per cent), but less so in Japan (46 per cent) and developing markets such as Latin America (48 per cent) and Asia (51 per cent).

- Just 32 per cent of people trust companies and brands.

- 54 per cent trust those that are socially and environmentally responsible.

Forbes magazine published figures[4] that support this as well:

- 87 per cent of global consumers believe that business needs to place at least equal weight on society's interests as on business' interests.

- 20 per cent of brands worldwide are seen to meaningfully and positively impact people's lives.

- Only 6 per cent of people believe the singular purpose of business is to make money for shareholders.

Brand Valuation consultants Millward Brown and former P&G global marketing officer Jim Stengel developed the list of 50 brands, which they say built the deepest relationships with customers while achieving the greatest financial growth from 2001 to 2011. To arrive at the Stengel 50,[5] they valued thousands of brands across 30+ countries. The list included both B2B and B2C businesses in 28 categories, ranging in size from $100 million in revenues to well over $100 billion.[6]

Investment in these companies – the 'Stengel 50' – over the past decade would have been 400 per cent more profitable than an investment in the S&P 500.[7]

Havas Global CEO (and co-founder of One Young World) David Jones provides three simple rules for Purpose-driven brands:[8]

1 *Forget 'image is everything' and embrace 'reality is everything.'*
Brands need to create a reality around what they do – it does not need to be perfect, but it does need to be honest.

2 *Do good to do well*. Old-world CSR saw companies 'give back' to society without a lot of concern about what they 'took out' (and how they took it out) in the first place. In the new world of Purpose-driven brands, how the business impacts its stakeholders internally and externally is baked into the operating model. Success generates profits that allow the organization to continue operating so long as its purpose remains relevant. Doing well is a by-product of doing 'good'.

3 *Outbehave the competition*. Eighty per cent of brand building is through behaviour, not marketing. People want to know what a company stands for, and they want to see evidence that the company is delivering on that promise.

Summary

Creating a strong, clear, compelling and credible Purpose for an organization that defines why it exists is critical for any organization that wants to enjoy longevity and relevance, not to mention resilience that leads to sustained performance. While an organization may or may not choose to explicitly use its purpose as its external positioning, it is worth considering. In any event, this Purpose should provide a clear compass that should guide the organization in:

- how it operates;
- what products and services it provides (and doesn't provide);
- what sectors and geographies it will (and will not) operate in;
- who it hires;
- who it fires;
- who it develops and how it develops and promotes them;
- what businesses it acquires;
- what assets it disposes of;
- how it manages its corporate responsibility efforts;
- how it markets and sells;
- how it engages with what stakeholders, when, why and how often;
- how it manages its supply chain;
- how it selects, manages and operates its facilities;
- who it lends to;

- who it borrows from;
- ... and so on.

In the next chapter we'll spend some time on Ambition – and its relationship to Purpose, Strategy and Proposition.

Notes

1   In fact, our initial model's fourth P was Positioning, not Proposition. It was only when we took the decision to commit to a Purpose-driven brand for one organization that it became clear that what we had defined as 'Positioning' was in fact a clearer articulation of the market-facing proposition and differentiator. This 'squared the circle' neatly in terms of the model's ability to deliver customer value propositions and employment value propositions driven by the same four-box model.

2   Kapelke, C (2013) The big ideal, *ANA Magazine*, Winter

3   Meaningful brands – Havas Media Group's metric of brand strength 2013

4   Mainwaring, S (2013) CMO vs CSO: 8 steps to bridge the divide that could undo your business, Forbes.com

5   Stengel, J (2011) *GROW: How ideals power growth and profit at the world's greatest companies*, Crown Business, New York

6   Millward Brown is to publish a book in October 2013 entitled *The Meaningful Brand* [Online] http://www.millwardbrown.com/Insights/PublishedBooks/The_Meaningful_Brand.aspx [accessed 11 October 2013]

7   King, B (2012) 50 fastest growing brands serve a 'higher purpose', sustainablebrands.com

8   Jones, D (2011) *Who Cares Wins*, Financial Times Series, Pearson Financial Times, Harlow, quoted by Lynn Satna Lucia in Kapelke (2013)

Ambition

10

أصحاب العقول العظيمة لديهم أهداف وغايات، أما الآخرون فيكتفون بالأحلام.أ
(واشطن إرفنج)

Great minds have goals and objectives, others just dreams
(WASHINGTON IRVING)[1]

AM•BI•TION /am'biSHən/*noun*

- A strong desire to do or to achieve something, typically requiring determination and hard work.
- Desire and determination to achieve success.

Why does 'Ambition' seem to have become a dirty word in some corners? Perhaps it's because some seem to have added '... at any cost and using any method' to the end of the definition. But if you combine Ambition with Purpose, it's an incredibly powerful combination.

Every organization should have an ambition: a clear picture of what it wishes to achieve. How this ambition interacts with the organization's purpose is critical; they are symbiotic.

Our model suggests a definition of ambition as: What do you want to achieve? What is the mountain you want to climb or the results that you want to achieve? There should be healthy, robust debate as you try to craft the two – often, ideas and content will change boxes several times before you become clear about the distinctions as a leadership team and as an organization.

If a purpose is *why* you exist, an ambition is *how* you measure your progress towards achieving that purpose. The best way to explore this dynamic is probably to show rather then tell, so here are some examples – some more financial than others. But as you can see, there is a clear balancing act between the Purposes and Ambitions. First, sometimes your ambition is something you don't share, or at least not fully, with the outside world – if it includes market share, revenue, profitability, growth or similar figures (IBM seems to fall into this category). Second, of course, of these examples the only one explicitly using the P-A-S-P model is EY, so some of these are 'reverse engineered!':

Unilever	Purpose:	'Create a better future every day.'
	Ambition:	• Help more than a billion people to improve their health and well-being.
		• Halve the environmental footprint of our products.
		• Source 100 per cent of our agricultural raw materials sustainably and enhance the livelihoods of people across our value chain.
SAP	Purpose:	'Helping the world run better.'
	Ambition:	SAP's integrated reporting[2] defines a range of financial and non-financial goals that include four key corporate objectives:

• Revenue
• Operating Margin
• Customer Access
• Employee Engagement

Four Environmental Indicators:
• Greenhouse Gas Footprint
• Total Energy Consumed
• Data Centre Energy
• Renewable Energy

And seven Social Indicators:
• Employee Engagement (also a corporate objective)
• Business Health Culture Index
• Employee Retention
• Women in Management
• Social Investment
• Capability Building
• Employer Ranking.

EY	Purpose:	'Building a better working world.'
	Ambition:[3]	By 2020 we will be a $50bn distinctive professional services organization:

- Best brand
- Most favoured employer
- Number 1 or 2 in market share in our chosen services
- Positive and strong relationships with all of our stakeholders.

Disney	Purpose:	'To always deliver, with integrity, the most exceptional entertainment experiences for people of all ages.'
	Ambition:	

- The company's primary financial goals are to maximize earnings and cash flow, and to allocate capital toward growth initiatives that will drive long-term shareholder value.
- Ultimately, our goal is to be the most admired company in the world. We believe we can achieve this goal by conducting our business and creating our products in an ethical manner, and by promoting the happiness and well-being of kids and families by inspiring them to join us in creating a brighter tomorrow.

McKinsey & Company	Purpose:	'World-changing client impact.'
	Ambition:	'To help leaders make distinctive, lasting, and substantial improvements in performance, and constantly build a great firm that attracts, develops, excites, and retains exceptional people.'

Harvard Business School Professor Mike Beer summarizes it well:[4]

We talk about one of the key disciplines: forging a strategic identity. It means that they start the process of deciding what they're going to do, what services or products they're going to offer, who they are, what markets they will go into, and what they're going to do from a business point of view, by first asking themselves, who are we? They start from the inside out, go out, rather than from the outside in.

So what do the worst firms on Wall Street do? They chase profits, profits that were not necessarily in their core area of capabilities or their long-term path. They just chase profits.

These firms don't chase profits. They expect profits. They get profits. But they start by saying who are we? What are the capabilities we have? What are people in our organization passionate about? What do we care about? What are our values? And then now let's find the intersect between market opportunities and who we are to take advantage.

Another discipline that these companies have is essentially creating a performance-driven culture. When things are tough, figuring out ways to do better in tough times, to be inventive, to be innovative about what they do is by essentially creating high standards and enrolling people in those high standards. Now how do they enroll people in the high standards? They enroll people in high standards by articulating a higher purpose.

So using that higher purpose, by people identifying with the company and seeing that it has a higher purpose beyond simply the financial results of the company, they also understand and want to enable the company to be successful in those shorter-term financial results. And as a result, they exert extra effort, more innovation, more problem solving to try to do the best they can in those tough times.

Summary

As you can see, the precise nature of your ambition and how it relates to your purpose can (and should) vary based on your own unique circumstances. Some organizations put in place very precise targets and metrics. Others put in place a time by which they wish to achieve the ambition, which allows it to flex without shifting the purpose (which should, of course, seldom if ever change). Some mix tangible financial elements with intangible 'social' elements – while others put very clear and firm objectives against each.

All of them seem to understand the notion of the desire, determination and hard work that it takes to succeed – while ensuring that such ambitions are in the context of a higher sense of purpose.

Notes

1   I discovered this quote originally in Arabic and its translation was perfect!

2   http://www.sapintegratedreport.com/2012/en/key-facts/connecting-financial-and-non-financial-performance.html [accessed 11 October 2013]

3   http://goingconcern.com/post/new-ey-50-billion-revenue-goal-squishy-independence-and-adios-ampersand [accessed 11 October 2013]

4   Quoted in HBR IdeaCast, 20 October 2011 by Mike Beer. Beer, M *et al* (2011) *Higher Ambition: How great leaders create economic and social value*, Harvard Business Press Books, Cambridge, MA

Strategy

11

> *Take time to deliberate, but when the time for action comes,*
> *stop thinking and go in.*
>
> **(NAPOLEON BONAPARTE)**

> *In preparing for battle I have always found that plans are*
> *useless, but planning is indispensable.*
>
> **(DWIGHT D EISENHOWER)**

What is the plan?

This is not a book on organizational strategy in terms of proposing a way to craft, refine and implement strategy, so we will not spend a lot of time on this particular topic.

Having said that, it is no good having an aspirational Purpose and an inspiring Ambition if you do not have a clear plan in which you, your people and your stakeholders have confidence.

We define Strategy as 'a set of defined key areas of activity that the organization will focus on delivering in order to achieve its purpose and ambition. Defined, measurable objectives (KPIs) and implementation action plans flow from the strategy.'

Depending on when you decide to address the Purpose, Ambition and Proposition model has a significant impact on the degree to which your strategy can be easily 'lifted and shifted' or whether it requires more significant consideration and revision. What generally happens is that in the process of developing a strategy, the requirement for being clear on Purpose and Ambition emerges. If these are not clear, generally a good strategy team will demand clarification from their peers, subordinates and boards.

The Purpose and Ambition can have a very positive impact on the articulation and categorization of a strategy – often providing the lens through which many disparate elements of strategy (ranging from service offerings to acquisition plans to IT and infrastructure to talent acquisition and management) can be put into clearer and more relevant buckets.

The power of having a clear purpose and ambition lies in the fact that it also helps highlight areas of strategy that are spurious and do not have a material impact on their achievement. The essence of strategy is choosing *what not to do*. 'Trade-offs are essential to strategy. They create the need for choice and purposefully limit what a company offers.'[1]

The business world, dynamic as it is, is also incredibly cyclical in terms of thinking and strategy. Although Porter's article[2] is nearly 20 years old, many organizations have lost sight of the idea of 'strategic fit' that sits, in many relevant ways, behind the four-box P-A-S-P model. Insofar as the model is intended to ensure that organizational activities are 'joined up' through all four boxes, Porter's observations on 'fit' still ring reassuringly true: that 'competitive advantage grows out of the entire system of activities; the whole matters more than any individual part'. He explores three kinds of strategic 'fit':

- *First-order fit* is ruthless consistency between the activity/function and the overall strategy. This ensures that the competitive advantages of activities do not erode or cancel themselves out.

- *Second-order fit* is when activities are reinforcing. This is achieved by ensuring operational and marketing activities that focus on a common need and align to common organizational, service and product design.

- *Third-order fit* is what Porter calls 'optimization of effort' and is focused on reduction of waste and wasted effort, coordination and information exchange across activities/functions.

'The more,' Porter concludes, 'a company's positioning relies on activities with second- and third-order fit, the more sustainable its advantage will be.'

Examples

Let's consider some examples to illustrate the point.

IBM

IBM's 'Solutions for a smarter planet' Purpose is no doubt aligned to an Ambition that is not shared externally (or at least not easily discovered!). However, its strategy is an exceptional example of how its strategy aligns to its purpose, and that it has clearly found a way to generate second- and third-level fit with its Purpose.

IBM has quite simply and clearly aligned the 10 areas where it sees data as being integral to creating solutions for a smarter planet, and turned them into strategic selling and service categories. While its 'go to market' structure, product and service are aligned to markets and sectors (eg Outsourcing, Consulting, IT services, Industry Solutions), it bases these on data-driven needs that help build a smarter planet – across a broad range of stakeholders:

The key areas that IBM highlights as their key service propositions and that support their overall purpose of creating a 'Smarter Planet' are all based on data capture. They are:

1 Smarter Analytics: *Turn Information into Insights*. IBM offers advanced analytics services that promise to guide businesses through the myriad of information sources they face on operating and strategic levels. This is where IBM comes in to facilitate optimum performance for its clients. Adequate data analysis guarantees smart, informed and fast decision-making processes.

2 Social Business: *Connect and Empower People*. IBM argues that through social collaboration comes innovation. By training its clients to embrace social technologies, a renewed approach to change and innovation is facilitated in which everyone along the supply chain is involved, from the employees to the suppliers, clients and top management.

3 Cloud Computing: *The Cloud Removes Restraints*. With the advent of smarter business come more data to store and more systems and processes to keep in mind. IBM's expertise lies in adequately managing the costs of maintaining these while also reducing and redistributing efforts. Utilizing the cloud becomes an integral step in ensuring a more efficient and lighter organization, which efficiently utilizes its technological resources.

4 Smarter Commerce: *Customers Come of Age*. Today's customers are savvier, more connected than ever before and keen to get transparent information and engagement with companies. IBM argues that with its commerce consultancy services, organizations will be able to keep track of consumers' demands, and engage with them on an authentic basis.

5   Mobile Enterprise: *Business Moves to Mobility.* One of the most revolutionary changes in today's business world is the rise of the mobile consumer. Armed with tablets and smart phones, consumers are able to browse, shop and pay for their shopping on the move. IBM's Mobility Enterprise Division looks at ensuring that businesses are ready to respond to consumers' desires to consume on the go.

6   Smarter Security: *Manage Risk, Security and Compliance.* Smarter businesses need to strive for more secure processes. With the threat of security, market, operational, environmental and compliance risks abreast, top management needs to be able to identify risks and propose a suitable response. IBM suggests systems improvements and efficient process changes to ensure that threats are mitigated and dealt with.

7   PureSystems and PureData: *Integrated Solutions Pave the Way.* IBM's systems team promises to ally individual technological requirements with systems solutions. By tailoring hardware and software into a single system specific to the organization, it pledges to reduce inefficiency and ensure top performance.

8   Smarter Computing: *Drive Entreprises' Effectiveness and Efficiency.* This is IBM's last operational consultancy arm, looking at improving day-to-day processes and systems. Smarter companies need to achieve more in a less-performing market.

Unilever

Unilever's strategy is famously aligned to its 'Sustainable Living Plan', where all brand and innovation activities are aligned to, and measured against, a core set of strategic milestones.

By aligning its actions with the aims of improving health and well-being, reducing environmental impact and enhancing livelihoods, Unilever strives to promote a sustainable future for both itself and the world it operates in. Initiatives to improve health and well-being include particular focus on hygiene and nutrition, while it strives to improve its environmental impact by looking at greenhouse gases, water and waste policies. Finally, Unilever looks to enhance livelihoods by putting in place sustainable sourcing and other livelihood initiatives (Table 11.1).

TABLE 11.1   Unilever's 'Sustainable Living Plan'

Key aim	Improving health and well-being	Reducing environmental impact	Enhancing livelihoods
Initiatives	Health, hygiene, nutrition	Greenhouse gases, water, waste	Sustainable sourcing, better livelihoods

While it could certainly be argued that Unilever no doubt has a robust set of operational and management processes, structures and approaches to delivery, CEO Paul Polman makes it very clear that the 'Sustainable Living Plan' is synonymous with its strategy.

EY

While we can assume that EY, like IBM and Unilever, also has deep and detailed execution plans within each element of its strategy, its three areas of focus are clearly lined up to its Purpose of 'Building a better working world' and the specific Ambitions it seeks to achieve by 2020. These are:[3]

- relentless focus on winning in the market;
- create the highest-performing teams;
- strengthen global, empower local.

Each of these three strategic pillars provides clear direction and clear priorities for anyone in the organization to assess their own efforts and activities against, particularly in reference to the Purpose and Ambition.

Summary

No business can create a sustainable strategy if that strategy is disconnected from a higher-order Purpose matched to a clear Ambition. Organizations may enjoy short-term periods of success, and indeed can often craft and execute effective strategies without having documented their purpose and ambition, but for the longer term there are clear benefits to be achieved and lessons to learn from the more integrated thinking proposed here.

The next chapter discusses Proposition – both customer and talent – before the final chapter on how to bring it all together into a cohesive Brand and Talent management approach.

Notes

1   Porter, M (1996) What is strategy?, *Harvard Business Review*, November–December

2   Porter, M (1996)

3   http://goingconcern.com/post/new-ey-50-billion-revenue-goal-squishy-independence-and-adios-ampersand [accessed 11 October 2013]

Proposition

12

In communication, as in architecture, less is more. You have to sharpen your message to cut into the mind. You have to jettison the ambiguities, simplify the message, and then simplify it some more if you want to make a long-lasting impression.

(AL RIES AND JACK TROUT)[1]

What is the deal?

Having defined, agreed and articulated Purpose, Ambition and Strategy, it's important to ensure that the Proposition – the deal on offer – to customers and to talent is lined up.

It's central to the P-A-S-P model that there is one core set of ideas that is then articulated and brought to life across the talent market and the customer marketplace.

Positioning

The P-A-S-P model uses the expression 'proposition' rather than 'positioning'. This is because an organization has choices to make in considering its *positioning* in the context of the P-A-S-P model. The proposition (for talent and customers) can be identical to the positioning, but it needs to be modulated for each audience.

It is useful to consider a spectrum of options when considering an organization's positioning. Since brand consideration and preference is generally seen to be as much a product of emotional decision making as rational decision making, brand positioning is typically approached using a considered blend of both rational and emotional elements and attributes.

According to recent research reported in *Psychology Today*,[2] built on decades of study:

- MRI neuro-imagery shows that when evaluating brands, people primarily use emotions (personal feelings and experiences) rather than information (brand attributes, features and facts).

- Advertising research reveals that emotional response has far greater influence on reported intent to buy a product than does the ad's content – by a factor of 3 to 1 for television commercials and 2 to 1 for print ads.

- The Advertising Research Foundation concluded that the emotion of 'likeability' is the measure most predictive of whether an advertisement will increase a brand's sales.

- Studies show that positive emotions towards a brand have far greater influence on loyalty than trust and other judgements which are based on a brand's attributes.

One way of viewing this is to use a continuum and to agree the most favourable positioning opportunity for the organization. This positioning decision must account for the authenticity of the positioning to the organization – it needs to be true; the relevance to the marketplace (talent, customers and stakeholders); and its differentiator from alternative providers of products, service and employment. There are many models, but one of the most effective is also one of the simplest. It's a simple continuum with rational positionings and emotional positionings at either extreme, with variations in between (Figure 12.1).

Infrastructure-led positioning

Location and time can drive powerful positions: mobile emergency car services, credit cards accepted at more locations, global reach are some examples. Such positions are generally built and protected through innovation or sheer mass and scale.

Product or service-led positioning

The organization can choose to position itself specifically around its customer value proposition. This is the most direct and relevant positioning

FIGURE 12.1 A brand positioning spectrum

Why	Who	How	What	Where/When
MORE EMOTIONAL AND INTANGIBLE				**MORE RATIONAL AND TANGIBLE**
Why	**Who**	**How**	**What**	**Where/When**
Purpose	**Values**	**Process**	**Product/Service**	**Infrastructure**
Why your organization does what it does as a driver of Awareness, Consideration, Preference and Advocacy	**Who** you and your people are as a driver of Awareness, Consideration, Preference and Advocacy	**How** your organization does what it does as a driver of Awareness, Consideration, Preference and Advocacy	**What** your organization does as a driver of Awareness, Consideration, Preference and Advocacy	**Where** and/or **When** your organization does what it does as a driver of Awareness, Consideration, Preference and Advocacy

from a commercial business perspective: the most authentic, relevant and differentiating elements of the product or service in relationship to its end user, customer or consumer. This relatively traditional positioning approach was developed in the late 1940s based on the concept of a 'unique selling proposition' (USP). Provided the product or service is difficult to duplicate, this positioning offers many benefits. The product can be homogeneous or premium, so long as the positioning allows a price premium. Having consistently innovative and market-leading phones and tablets is one example; having the most low-cost alternative could be another. Both have their place.

Process-led positioning

Having a unique, bespoke process that allows for differentiation – the product or service might be similar to the competition, but the unique way the organization goes about delivering it allows for a competitive advantage which allows the organization to generate enhanced margin. Trade-marked solutions or a difficult-to-duplicate approach works here – for example, in the international overnight delivery category.

Values-led positioning

A positioning based on the values of an organization and its people can provide a good platform for positioning, particularly in the services or professional services sector. Locations, services and processes might be similar, but the kind of person the organization attracts and how it approaches service delivery are key.

Purpose-led positioning

The sense of 'why' the organization does what it does, as opposed to what, how, who, when and where it does what it does, can drive significant benefits. Using this as the driver of positioning can have long-term benefits, as discussed in Chapter 9. It can also raise challenges, on the other hand, insofar as it can be challenging to activate such a positioning in the day-to-day delivery of the product and service.

In positioning, there is no place on the spectrum that is inherently more favourable or less favourable than others. It is more important that the organization identifies the positioning that it can occupy with the greatest confidence as it balances authenticity, relevance and differentiation. In the P-A-S-P model, positioning might express itself with the greatest relevance in day-to-day operations at the Proposition level – while it can also be driven by the overarching sense of Purpose. Some organizations consciously decide to balance both, using a higher sense of Purpose at the corporate level, and more tangible propositions at the market-facing customer and talent levels – without creating confusion or conflict. The key, of course, is to have it all align.

In theory, then, the overarching Purpose could serve to enhance Awareness and Consideration, while the more granular propositions for customers and talent serve to enhance Preference. Delivering on *both* promises will then create stronger Preference and Advocacy. In this way the model operates comprehensively – so the strategy can use Positioning and Proposition to achieve the Ambition (Figure 12.2).

FIGURE 12.2   How P-A-S-P drives Awareness, Consideration, Preference and Advocacy

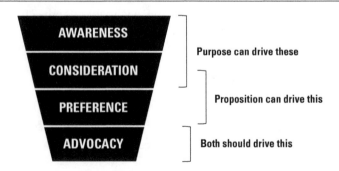

Proposition

Once the positioning has been agreed, it should provide a clear road map to develop sharp and clearly articulated propositions for the talent and customer marketplaces. These propositions are based on the *same* Purpose and are aimed at achieving the *same* Ambition for the organization, and must be explicitly aligned to, and encapsulated within, the Strategy.

Customer value proposition

We define customer value proposition as:

> A statement that defines the point of competitive advantage of the brand, rationally and emotionally – what makes it distinctive and special in the minds of customers and can be succinctly expressed as its 'Differentiator' or its 'Positioning'.

The customer value proposition should be rooted in the positioning selected and crafted in relationship to the Purpose, Ambition and Strategy.

Employment value proposition

We define the employment value proposition as:

> A statement that defines what makes the organization a desirable place to work and what differentiates it from other organizations – it clarifies the 'give and get' of the employment deal. It performs best when it is seamlessly connected to the employee experience before, during and after their association with the organization.

The employment value proposition should be authentic, relevant and differentiated, rather than seek to be all things to all people. It must also reflect the Purpose, Ambition and Strategy and be relevant to future talent across all touch points in the employee lifecycle explored in Chapter 7:

- entry level;
- graduate;
- experienced hires;
- senior executives.

It should also be relevant to existing employees, and should therefore be integrated into ongoing talent management and engagement efforts:

- pre-joining experience;
- onboarding experience and activities;
- career planning;
- learning and development;
- reward and recognition (compensation, benefits, awards, incentives);
- sales and marketing processes and training;
- customer service processes and training.

Some examples are provided in the next chapter, which discusses how to try to bring these elements together in a sensible, coordinated and, ideally, simpler manner.

Notes

1   Ries, A and Trout, J (1981) *Positioning: The battle for your mind,* McGraw-Hill, New York

2   Murray, P (2013) Inside the consumer mind: how emotions influence how we buy, *Psychology Today*, February. Research informed by Damasio, A (2005) *Descartes' Error: Emotion, reason and the human brain*, Penguin Books, Harmondsworth

Putting it all together

13

> *You can't stay in your corner of the forest waiting for others to come to you. You have to go to them sometimes.*
>
> **(A A MILNE, 1882–1956)**

Putting P-A-S-P to work

The previous chapters outlined the P-A-S-P model overall and provided some guidance on how to get an organization aligned around the core set of concepts:

- Purpose
- Ambition
- Strategy
- Proposition.

In most organizations, that exercise in itself can pose significant challenges and often takes at least three months and typically longer in a larger, complex global enterprise. Getting a leadership team from functions to go-to-market units aligned is no small feat. But once the framework has been populated, that's only the beginning.

The next requirement is equally if not more challenging: getting everyone in the organization with a role relating to delivering the talent or customer experience, and communicating and engaging with stakeholders internally and externally, to follow it. Like Porter says:[1] It is as much about what you *don't* do and say as it is about what you *do* say and do. This means, more often than not, undertaking a 'stop, continue/evolve, start' exercise across critical business and communication processes and functions.

Friction points

One of the key friction points in the exercise is, as you have probably guessed, in the overlap between brand and marketing activities (which are traditionally seen as customer and external stakeholder facing), and human resources activities (which are traditionally seen as future and present talent facing – both internal and external). It's often a lack of clarity around the core idea, a culture of separating these activities or, at best, working cross-functionally to align them. However, such activities typically solve short-term brand and talent marketing and communication requirements over a relatively short period. Over the longer term, this separation almost inevitably leads to increasing fragmentation of messaging – creating legacy issues that can entrench perspectives and constrain your ability to build and defend brand value in the aggregate.

It's a difficult challenge for both functional perspectives. Typically, brand and marketing are seen to lack the expertise in talent management and the employee engagement insights and technical processes to be able to drive the best results. At the same time, human resources and talent acquisition and management experts are often seen to lack the clarity and business pragmatism required to simplify – or at least synthesize – external imperatives and strategic business drivers. This all too often creates a stand-off where each perspective struggles to find a common ground. This can lead to sub-optimizing the end result for both stakeholders: all too often the result is a compromise.

What also complicates the situation is that an industry has grown up around human resources and talent acquisition: 'employer branding' as a solution that provides an avenue for the talent side of the equation to create its own subset of rules, models, terms and both internal and external engagement efforts. It is an idea that is seductive and attractive, not least because it acts as a pressure valve to mitigate the friction between HR and marketing. With fast-moving, dynamic business environments and time pressure, it is not surprising that organizations 'throw in the towel' and avoid conflict in order to get on with the job at hand – running a successful, sustainable operation.

Is employer branding the right approach any more?

The 'employer branding' approach served an important purpose during the previous decade, mitigating the tensions among functions and allowing a more thoughtful and robust approach to the increasingly critical challenge of attracting, recruiting, engaging, developing, retaining and eventually exiting the best possible talent for an organization. And it is still critical – based on the previous chapter – to be crystal clear on the employment (talent) value proposition aligned to the external value proposition.

But there have been massive changes in the recruitment industry overall – particularly the recruitment marketing world, where employer branding has become a staple of the industry. The hard reality is that the shift to technology, social media, fragmentation of media and easy access to information by all stakeholders – in this case, importantly, future, present and past talent – has all but eliminated the traditional recruitment marketing industry. Traditional display advertising, job boards and on-campus approaches are no longer as viable as they once were. These stakeholders – just like others – now have access to the widest possible range of resources in finding out about your organization. So having a careers site and a presence on sites like Facebook and, more importantly, LinkedIn are all critically important.

Despite the importance of having a clear, compelling, relevant, authentic and differentiating talent proposition, the risk is that it has too little connection or no clear line of sight to the overall brand. In some cases, the employment proposition can actually compete with, or even contradict, key elements of the customer brand positioning!

One brand

Ultimately, an organization has only one brand. This is its reputation, in the aggregate, across all stakeholders.

For some stakeholders – in particular, the ones who provide the investment for the organization to sustain itself, and the ones it needs to attract, motivate and retain in order to do that – there might be variations on the messaging, and slightly different perceptions of what the organization is, what it does and what it stands for. And while there will be a degree of variation between, for example, the reputation of a fast-moving consumer goods (FMCG) company vs an energy company vs a professional services firm, there must be an overarching alignment of the brand for all stakeholders.

As someone who has been a long-time practitioner and proponent of employer branding, it strikes me that the evolution of employer branding has come full circle. It no longer seems that 'traditional' employer-branding approaches that have entered mainstream practice will advance the brand agenda, the talent agenda, or drive sustainable business growth.

Having helped to develop and drive successful employment value propositions for some of the world's leading companies across sectors under the employer-branding banner, that might come as a surprise. As a pioneer of connecting employer-branding efforts to internal employee engagement efforts as well, however, it has become clear that the 'cottage industry' of employer branding could now well be doing as much damage to brand equity as it is helping to create awareness and differentiation in various talent markets. Time and time again we are seeing the Huawei example being played out in internal communications, employee engagement and recruitment marketing.

It's got to stop, and the time is now. In short, we need to stop thinking about 'brand' as a marketing priority and 'employer brand' as an HR and talent priority. They are of equal importance, they need to be aligned, and it should no longer be a sense of an uneasy alliance as it can often seem to be.

The degree to which an employment value proposition aligns to the consumer and corporate brands can be debated. For example, you wouldn't dream of aligning the employment value proposition for someone working for an FMCG company selling chewing gum to the product brand proposition. However, you would certainly want the product brand proposition to be supportive of the corporate Purpose, Ambition, Strategy and Positioning. And you would want the employment value proposition aligned to the same thing. For a service organization – whether in hospitality or professional services – it is even more important for the employment value proposition to be closely aligned, since the brand experience is by and large delivered by people.

Looking at it from the opposite angle, how strange would it be for a company reliant on its people to deliver the brand experience to have radically different sets of values, attributes and communications in the talent market?

The conclusion is that it's time to rethink the degree to which you invest resource in employer branding as a separate activity distinct from customer branding. There is a distinction to be made between creating an impactful employment value proposition that can drive short-, medium- and long-term recruitment media (marketing and communications) campaigns, and creating what many might say is a 'competing' brand due to functional silos. You want your employer brand to be woven into your corporate brand; your reputation as an employer should be a core element of your reputation as an organization – not a separate set of attributes.

In short: you have one brand. Your future, current and past talent are a stakeholder group to a greater or lesser degree of comparable importance to your customer audience. While you certainly want to modulate the messaging and engagement methodology for both audiences, it would be very inefficient to develop separate brand positionings and equity in different 'brands' for customer and talent audiences. Fewer brands are always less expensive and more efficient to build and defend than multiple brands.

In other words, maybe it's time to 'zag' while everyone else 'zigs' as they hop merrily aboard the employer brandwaggon.

The integrated approach

If you have any doubts about the market's view on integration, consider this. An ISBA (Incorporated Society of British Advertisers) sponsored survey conducted by Professor Jonathan Lace[2] found:

- The average client has seven different agencies.
- One in ten retains eleven or more agencies.
- One-third of clients surveyed believe that their *external* resource structure is characterized by silo thinking.
- Even more clients believe that their external resources are characterized by silo activity.
- Typically each agency/discipline is unsure what others are doing.

In a survey of 46 global marketers conducted by Flock Associates:[3]

- 70 per cent said they would get a 10 per cent greater return on their marketing investment if their campaigns were better integrated.

- 31 per cent said they would get a 20 per cent greater return on their marketing investment if their plans were better integrated.

- 64 per cent said their agencies were poor at collaborating to find production efficiency for the client.

Network analysis

Another interesting and informative proof point that supports the notion that the era of silos needs to come crashing down is a look at the network/social network analysis work done both internally within organizations and externally across the various social listening platforms. Network analysis describes social and technical resources within and between businesses. The nodes in a value network represent people (or roles). The nodes are connected by interactions that represent tangible and intangible deliverables. These deliverables take the form of knowledge or other intangibles and/or financial value. Value networks exhibit interdependence. They account for the overall worth of products and services. Companies have both internal and external value networks.[4]

In what can only be described as a less-than-shocking revelation, these studies demonstrate that people inside and outside organizations tend to have regular contact and deep working relationships outside their immediate function or specialist area of expertise. In fact, in populations of industries where this is less apparent (remember our discussion about diversity?), performance, innovation and engagement are hindered.[5] One example, taken from my personal experience, is within professional associations. When they become too inwardly focused and talk only about the competencies and approaches to practising their craft – whether brain surgery or employee communications – they cut off external perspectives and the diversity needed to drive innovation. By and large in the employee communications arena, this has, sadly, been the case for more than a decade – with little evidence of innovation and a preponderance of only incremental 'best practice' improvements to existing methods.[6]

By now your understanding of the P-A-S-P model should demonstrate that its power lies in its *integrative* nature. If properly developed, it should render 'rogue' communications difficult to justify in *both* the brand/marketing and the HR/talent spaces, since both will have clearly marked propositions that are aligned to the Purpose, Ambition and Strategy (Figure 13.1).

As you can imagine, changing a small part of the Purpose, Ambition,

FIGURE 13.1   The P-A-S-P model

PURPOSE	AMBITION	STRATEGY	PROPOSITION
Why you exist	What you aim to achieve	Your plan to get there	How you best express it

Top line: A concise 5-word version	**Top line:** 3 (+/–2) goals – financial or otherwise	**Top line:** 3 (+/–2) activities operations align to	**Top line:** A concise 5–10-word version
Elevator pitch: A 100-word version	**Elevator pitch:** A 20–30-word version for each	**Elevator pitch:** A 30–100-word version for each	**Elevator pitch:** A 100-word version
Deep dive: As long as you and your audience find interesting and useful	**Deep dive:** As long as you and your audience find interesting and useful	**Deep dive:** As long as you and your audience find interesting and useful	**Deep dive:** As long as you and your audience find interesting and useful

Strategy or Proposition will force changes in other parts of the model – it is an adaptive system. So, for example, if the Strategy is amended to account for 'Ensuring attraction and development of the best talent in the sector', then:

- The Ambition may need to be amended to reflect the desire to become the most favourable employer.

- The employment value proposition will need to ensure that it makes clear that only top-tier talent are suitable.

- The Purpose will need to be considered in terms of its attractiveness to the best talent in the market.

The benefit of operating P-A-S-P as a set of integrated moving parts is that it forces executives and leaders to ensure that the interests and objectives of the organization – not specific elements within it – are at the heart of decisions.

Although not all of the organizations in the example (Figure 13.2) used this model, I have retrofitted them to the model to include publicly available information to demonstrate how improved alignment can result.

FIGURE 13.2 Some examples

	PURPOSE Why you exist	AMBITION What you aim to achieve	STRATEGY Your plan to get there	PROPOSITION How you best express it
IBM	To provide solutions for a smarter planet	Not public – however: • Improve gross margin year on year	Focus on the 8–10 markets where data is at the heart of customer needs – drive growth, manage risk, optimize performance	Customers: Let's build a smarter planet. Talent: Help us build a smarter planet.
Amazon	We seek to be Earth's most customer-centric company	Not public – however: Be the first choice for four primary customer sets: consumers, sellers, enterprises, and content creators	• Relentless focus on customer service • Emphasis on the long term • Bold investments • Maximize future cash flow • Weigh compensation via stock options over cash	Customers: Obsess over customers. Talent: Work hard, have fun, make history. (You must think like, and therefore must actually be, an owner.)
EY	Building a better working world	• Revenue target • Best brand • Market share target • Employer of choice • Earnings	• Relentless focus on the market • Highest-performing teams • Strengthen global, empower local	Customers: Exceptional Client Service from High Performance Teams. Talent: No matter when you join or how long you stay, the exceptional EY experience will last a lifetime.
Johnson & Johnson	Caring for the world, one person at a time	• The J&J Credo	• To create value through innovation • To extend our global reach, with local focus • To execute with excellence in everything we do • Imperatives: Connect, Shape, Lead, Deliver	Customers: By caring, one person at a time, we help billions of people around the world live longer, healthier and happier lives. Talent: Every invention, every product, and every breakthrough to human health and well-being has been powered by people.

It applies to every function

While we have focused on the most visible functional alignment issues –
marketing and HR – the same applies to other functions in the business.
In particular, Finance, Corporate Responsibility and Supply Chain must
also be aligned to the P-A-S-P model in order to ensure that what you
SAY is always reflected in what you DO (Table 13.1).

TABLE 13.1   Examples of alignment to P-A-S-P

Function	Process/Policy/ Topic	Alignment
Talent acquisition	Employment Value Proposition	• Explicit, unambiguous alignment to Purpose • Clarity regarding how Talent fits into Strategy • Explicit explanation of how Talent contributes to Ambition
Talent engagement	Brand engagement	• Describes P-A-S-P • Makes each relevant, individually and as a unit, to departments, functions, teams and individuals • Connects internal world to external world
Talent management	Development, Competencies, Reward and recognition	• Legacy 'standalone' initiatives/ approaches must be evolved to align to P-A-S-P • Competency frameworks and career paths revisited and realigned to P-A-S-P
Sponsorships	Global and local efforts to align brand with third parties	• Sponsorships must be evaluated in line with P-A-S-P • May require stopping some and starting others

TABLE 13.1   *continued*

Function	Process/Policy/ Topic	Alignment
Corporate Responsibility / CSR	Workplace, Marketplace, Community and Environmental activities	• Activities that do not explicitly align to P-A-S-P should be re-evaluated and possibly stopped • All activities must be explicitly aligned to P-A-S-P
Strategic investment and acquisition	Operations to acquire, transform, divest	• Any operation must be reviewed in line with its fit across P-A-S-P
Products and Services	Market-facing revenue-generating activities	• Existing services should be aligned to P-A-S-P • P-A-S-P should serve as an explicit driver of service and product innovation
Environments / Facilities	Offices, retail spaces	• Talent, customer and stakeholder touch points should represent P-A-S-P
Suppliers / Supply Chain	Who provides services to help you run your business	• Suppliers should be vetted against their alignment and appropriateness in terms of P-A-S-P
Finance	Investment management, investment guidance, borrowing, paying	• P-A-S-P should act as a guide for BAU and other key finance decisions and practices

Testing the approach

If the overall process introduced via the P-A-S-P model is followed, it should prove relatively easy to 'test' whether communications and processes – in whole or in individual elements – are aligned to it as a core platform. You will have generated:

- internal leadership, management and employee insight;
- customer and other stakeholder insight;
- an audit of your own communication ecosystem – messages and channels – internally and externally;
- a competitive analysis of both customer and talent markets;
- a Purpose, Ambition, Strategy and Proposition set that has been tested and, ideally, co-created with these stakeholders;
- core message frameworks including proof points and reasons to believe for your key constituent groups;
- a decision on positioning that is reflected in customer and employment value propositions.

Any existing or new communication or process should be measured against, and aligned to, the P-A-S-P model. If there is no fit or poor alignment, whether to proceed with the communication or process should be seriously debated.

Summary

Like any model, P-A-S-P is only as good as the engagement that surrounds it and the intention of all participants to arrive at the best result for the organization. In our experience, the model has proven to be immensely valuable as a framework for the conversation and debate, a 'terminology neutral' container for existing thinking and as strong an approach as any to gaining leadership, management, employee and stakeholder buy-in relating to a significant strategic refresh or repositioning exercise.

It can also serve as a powerful set of guiding principles to ensure clarity and alignment to organizational change and transformation efforts. It can help define what should stay, what should go, and what should be re-evaluated. Surely, in the fast-moving, always-on, dynamic and unpredictable global economy, that ought to be of value to everyone in every organization.

Notes

1   Porter, M (1996) What is strategy?, *Harvard Business Review*, November–December

2   For more details on the ISBA research, visit http://www.advertising-research.com/smcrindex.htm [accessed 11 October 2013]

3   Flock is an agency specializing in helping clients with integrated marketing – see http://www.flock-associates.com [accessed 11 October 2013]

4   http://en.wikipedia.org/wiki/Value_network [accessed 11 October 2013]

5   Stabell, C and Fjeldstad, Ø (1998) Configuring value for competitive advantage: on chains, shops, and networks, *Strategic Management Journal*, May

6   A very rough qualitative analysis of the association conference industry across North America, Europe and Asia indicated that the speakers, presentations and core topics across internal communications, employee engagement, brand engagement and employer branding have been virtually unchanged since 1999. The only potential exception has been the (arguably opportunistic in many cases) connection of employer branding to internal employee engagement.

Toolkit

14

We become what we behold.
We shape our tools and then our tools shape us.
(MARSHALL MCLUHAN)

This section includes some worksheets you can use to explore the potential of the P-A-S-P approach advocated in this book. Feel free to use these or modify them for non-commercial (eg internal, non-fee-generating consultancy) purposes.

Exercise one: Value disciplines

This exercise is a powerful one to stimulate debate among your leadership team across all functions. It's very simple:

1 Each individual (or small team) is allocated an imaginary budget of $100.

2 The $100 represents the level of priority investment they believe should be made into the delivery of what the organization does.

3 There are three categories they are allowed to invest in (see below).

4 The challenge: you give the team (theoretically or otherwise) one $50 bill and ten $5 bills. You can't make change. So you have to put half your cash on one of the value disciplines and spread the rest between the other two.

5 The teams discuss and debate their investment, and then they must present back to the group:

   – How did we arrive at this investment decision?

   – Where was the greatest level of debate – and why?

- – What are the general learnings and implications?
- – What are the implications for reputation management?
- – What are the implications for how we attract talent?
- – What are the implications for how we engage, retain and reward talent?

Categories

FIGURE 14.1   Value disciplines

Product/Service Leadership	Customer/ Market Intimacy	Operational Excellence/ Efficiency
Investing in this category means that efforts are focused not on efficiency or consumer/market insight, but on crafting the **best possible level of quality in delivering whatever the consumer or client pays for**.	Investing in this category means that efforts are **focused on research and innovation driver by broad and deep understanding of the customer and their market.**	Investing in this category means that efforts are focused on **improving efficiency and processes throughout the delivery of the product or service**. It means reduced focus on customer service or insight, and a tolerance for a product/ service that is not differentiated from the competition.

• How did we arrive at this investment decision? • Where was the greatest level of debate – and why? • What are the general learnings and implications?	• What are the implications for reputation management? • What are the implications for how we attract talent? • What are the implications for how we engage, retain and reward talent?

Category one: product/service leadership

Investing in this category means that efforts are focused not on efficiency or consumer/market insight, but on crafting the best possible level of quality in delivering whatever the consumer or client pays for. This requires focus on the core processes of invention, product development and market exploitation. Some typical attributes are:[1]

- a business structure that is loosely knit, ad hoc, and ever-changing to adjust to entrepreneurial initiatives and redirections that characterize working in unexplored territory;

- management systems that are results driven, that measure and reward new product success and that don't punish the experimentation needed to get there;

- a culture that encourages individual imagination, accomplishment, out-of-the-box thinking and a mindset driven by the desire to create the future.

Category two: operational excellence

Investing in this category means that efforts are focused on improving efficiency and processes throughout the delivery of the product or service. It means reduced focus on customer service or insight, and a tolerance for a product/service that is not differentiated from the competition. This requires focus on processes for end-to-end product supply and basic service that are optimized and streamlined to minimize cost and provide hassle-free service. Some typical attributes are:[2]

- operations that are standardized, simplified, tightly controlled and centrally planned, leaving few decisions to rank-and-file employees;

- management systems that focus on integrated, reliable, high-speed transactions and compliance to norms;

- a culture that abhors waste and rewards efficiency.

Category three: customer/marketplace intimacy

Investing in this category means that efforts are focused on research and innovation driven by broad and deep understanding of the customer and their market. This requires focus on the core processes of solution development (helping the customer understand exactly what is needed), results management (ensuring that the solution gets implemented properly) and relationship management. Some typical attributes are:[3]

- a business structure that delegates decision making to employees who are close to the customer;

- management systems that are geared towards creating results for carefully selected and nurtured clients;

- a culture that embraces specific rather than general solutions and thrives on deep and lasting client relationships.

FIGURE 14.2   A brand positioning spectrum

(dotted lines filling upper portion of figure)

MORE EMOTIONAL AND INTANGIBLE ←————————————————→ **MORE RATIONAL AND TANGIBLE**

Why	Who	How	What	Where/When
Purpose	**Values**	**Process**	**Product/Service**	**Infrastructure**
Why your organization does what it does as a driver of Awareness, Consideration, Preference and Advocacy	**Who** you and your people are as a driver of Awareness, Consideration, Preference and Advocacy	**How** your organization does what it does as a driver of Awareness, Consideration, Preference and Advocacy	**What** your organization does as a driver of Awareness, Consideration, Preference and Advocacy	**Where** and/or **When** your organization does what it does as a driver of Awareness, Consideration, Preference and Advocacy

Exercise two: Positioning

This spectrum (Figure 14.2) can be used in a number of ways. One approach is to identify the total number of attributes that you want to associate to your organization, and then plot them against this spectrum to assess their best fit and identify any clear centre of gravity.

Another approach is to use your Proposition or hypothetical propositions and plot them against the spectrum to assess their fit (in line with Purpose, Ambition and Strategy).

A third approach is to generate specific examples of products, services, communications, and other tangible organizational outputs and plot them against the continuum to see where your current activities tend to cluster (or not, as the case may be).

Ultimately this should shape your P-A-S-P model at the most fundamental and profound level.

FIGURE 14.3   Purpose, Ambition, Strategy, Proposition

PURPOSE	AMBITION	STRATEGY	PROPOSITION
Why you exist	What you aim to achieve	Your plan to get there	How you best express it

Top line: A concise 5-word version	**Top line:** 3 (+/–2) goals – financial or otherwise	**Top line:** 3 (+/–2) activities operations align to	**Top line:** A concise 5–10-word version
Elevator pitch: A 100-word version	**Elevator pitch:** A 20–30-word version for each	**Elevator pitch:** A 30–100-word version for each	**Elevator pitch:** A 100-word version
Deep dive: As long as you and your audience find interesting and useful	**Deep dive:** As long as you and your audience find interesting and useful	**Deep dive:** As long as you and your audience find interesting and useful	**Deep dive:** As long as you and your audience find interesting and useful

Exercise three: Purpose, Ambition, Strategy, Positioning

It takes the entire contents of all the work you have done within the context of this book to populate the framework shown in Figure 14.3. Its power is in its clarity and simplicity. There is no single correct answer for any organization; the key is to find the combination of elements that serves to unite, and to clearly, coherently and confidently tell your story.

Exercise four: Stakeholders

A stakeholder mapping exercise is important for any brand, talent or strategy management exercise. It can be as detailed or as top level as required. Figures 14.4 to 14.9 comprise a simple template for a stakeholder mapping exercise.

FIGURE 14.4 Stakeholder mapping – your organization

Stakeholder	Description	What is their interest, influence, stake?
Senior executives and leaders		
Business and people managers		
Employees – particularly new starters (and their families and friends)		
Contractors (and their families and friends)		
Former employees (alumni)		
Future (potential) employees		

FIGURE 14.5 Stakeholder mapping – third-party organizations

Stakeholder	Description	What is their interest, influence, stake?
Outsourced functions (HR, IT, etc)		
Suppliers		
Partners		
Regulators and government and related bodies		
Media and analysts		
NGOs and third sector		

FIGURE 14.6   Stakeholder mapping – the broader community

Stakeholder	Description	What is their interest, influence, stake?
The investment community		
Shareholders/ investors		
Environmental and corporate responsibility interests		
Special interest groups		

FIGURE 14.7 Stakeholder mapping – customers/clients

Stakeholder	Description	What is their interest, influence, stake?
Potential customers or clients		
Existing customers or clients		
Past customers or clients		

FIGURE 14.8   Stakeholder mapping – competitors

Stakeholder	Description	What is their interest, influence, stake?
Direct/traditional		
Indirect/ non-traditional		
Competitors for key talent		

FIGURE 14.9 Stakeholder mapping – stakeholders

Stakeholder	Description	What is their interest, influence, stake?

FIGURE 14.10   Blank messaging framework

OVERARCHING MESSAGE		
KEY MESSAGE 1	KEY MESSAGE 2	KEY MESSAGE 3
Proof point 1 Proof point 2 Proof point 3	Proof point 1 Proof point 2 Proof point 3	Proof point 1 Proof point 2 Proof point 3

Exercise five: Messaging framework

Once you have developed your Purpose, Ambition, Strategy and Proposition and identified the influence, interests and role of your stakeholders, you can use this simple tool (Figure 14.10) to develop messaging.

Typically organizations have a single 'master' set of messages, and often they develop subsets for specific audiences. The key, of course, is to make sure that the messages align. A subset of an overarching key message must be explicitly locked to the overarching key message – in many cases, it should even be the same.

Then it is important to define the key supporting messages, and to begin populating the reasons to believe and proof points for each. Ideally, you should have at least three relevant proof points for each supporting message.

A message framework serves as a guide, particularly when in doubt about the best way to approach how to communicate a topic or an opportunity.

Exercise six: Bringing it all together

The final analysis needs to be a strategic review that ensures that your Purpose, Ambition, Strategy and Proposition:

1 align to and reflect your Values;

2 are Authentic, Relevant for all stakeholders – and differentiated from your competition for both business and talent;

3 provide clear signposts, evidence and calls to action for each audience to drive Advocacy in a measurable manner (Figure 14.11).

FIGURE 14.11 Master P-A-S-P model

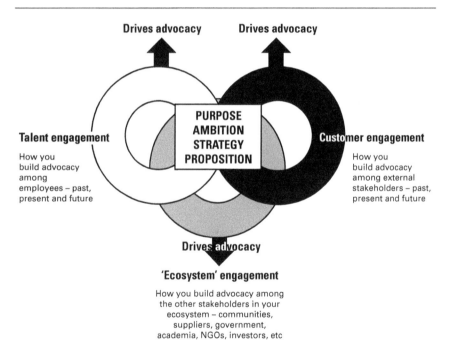

Notes

1 Treacy, M and Wiersema, F (1995) *The Discipline of Market Leaders*, Addison-Wesley, Wokingham

2 Treacy, M and Wiersema, F (1995)

3 Treacy, M and Wiersema, F (1995)

PART FOUR
Insight interviews

Brand and executive talent – Bob Benson

15

Bob Benson is one of the leading figures in the executive search industry, having served as a senior leader with Spencer Stewart and carried out a variety of roles internationally. He talks here about how to make sure that C-level and other senior hires can be aligned to the brand and talent agenda.

To what degree does brand enter the conversation when recruiting at the 'extreme' senior level?

It's one of the first things that come on the radar screen with any executive considering a move: what will this do for my personal reputation and will this client or company enhance my personal standing in the executive community?

The way we refer to it is crude but you have A players, B players and C players on the talent side and on the company side. Many times C players had aspirations to attract A player talent, but typically this won't happen unless it is a very special set of circumstances.

Brand plays an important part because you're consistently matching up the reputation or the personal brand of the talent with the brand of the client. Occasionally you will get an A player who sees something they like in the way the board is looking to take a B-level firm forward; then you might be able to then attract an A-level player into it.

To what degree do you ever see deals that look great on paper but the culture just isn't right? How did you manage that?

What an executive recruiter is paid to do is break the role into three categories: can-do, will-do and fit.

Can-do is the skills, experience and education the person should ideally have to perform the role. The will-do has to do with the type of organization. It might be a maintenance environment where you don't want to shake the trees or change things very much. It takes a certain type of person with a certain temperament and disposition to manage a maintenance environment. You don't want a high-growth type of individual, somebody that's looking to grow, grow, grow. Then there is growth: a lot of technology or new product companies are looking for somebody that can run them as fast as you can go to grow the top line.

The third type is turnaround, companies that are troubled for whatever reason whether it's financial or legal or any number of other reasons. They need a person that can come in and make a difference by shaking the trees.

The values and the skill set that is needed are very different in each environment. You can't put a maintenance manager into a turnaround situation and you can't put a turnaround person into a maintenance situation. It will just raise absolute havoc with the organization – and the individual will certainly fail; they'll be out looking for replacement soon.

What about the culture fit part of it?

You really have to get inside the organization and talk to a broad range of people to understand how they think, how they express themselves about any range of things from their social conscience to their environmental positions to their view of people to their determination to squeeze every potential penny of profit out of the organization.

What you hear is the way people describe events, situations handling people, handling customers, etc. You begin to understand how a business thinks and what they value.

It's not unusual for somebody to say: 'We're a highly ethical company. We believe in treating our employees with a great deal of respect. We're committed to their personal development.' After you've talked to 8, 10, 12 different people, you begin to hear the themes which start to make up what you'd call culture.

The similarities and the way people describe things begin to shape a picture of the kind of person that you would need. If you've got a company that is very concerned about people, how they're treated, fairness and developmental oriented, you would never take an executive who said 'people are just a cost, one of my resources, and if I haven't got the right ones I'll change them tomorrow'. You're not going to put that kind of individual into a company that has strong people-orientation. You learn when you know you've got the glove that fits the hand that the client is looking for.

So it's all about can-do, will-do and fit. It's easy to find the can-do. The others are a bit harder.

Are there situations where you deliberately put in a CEO to drive a different culture, or is that just a recipe for disaster?

Our job as a recruiter is to validate what a client is looking for to understand whether it exists and to help them understand the implications of the decision. You are always challenging your client against the realities of the marketplace, affordability and attractability. You have to educate your client to the fact that perfection doesn't exist and help them understand the trade-offs they're going to have to make.

You've got to bring to them a variety of people and different levels of experience. Those different levels of experience have different price tags connected with them.

You've worked internationally. Is there cultural variation when it comes to finding the right senior talent?

The decision process is very different. If you look at European companies, they have a governing structure that can be intertwined in a way that most US companies have stopped. You will find vastly different approaches in India versus former Soviet bloc countries and everywhere in between.

A big issue right now is that we are in a global economy and trying to find board leadership who can contribute across multiple cultures and geographies, and that is a serious challenge. Even with simple time zones and commitments within one region, business dealings become very difficult. One of the most taxing problems we're facing right now is that none of us sits in isolation any more.

So we may have different governance structures and different decision processes but the bottom line is: We're in a single global economy and we need to better understand the cultural differences of doing business and reading the nuances. In particular, US companies have not been terribly good at doing this on a global basis.

Diversity is a huge issue. What are your thoughts on how organizations are either tackling this or failing to tackle it when you look at female CEOs and female representatives at C-level and on boards?

There's been pretty poor performance on that. There are some signs that it is finally changing.

The 'boys' clubs' and the 'fraternities' and the 'private societies' of men are slowly being penetrated and there have been a lot of studies, especially in Scandinavia and Europe, about companies with higher numbers of women on their boards performing significantly better than companies with fewer. I still think there's a long way to go. Looking at support systems for one another the way men have supported one another over the years is key.

It's all about leadership, support and mentorship. You've got to have the sponsor and you've got to have the mentors and these things are just beginning to happen to the degree that they're going to make a difference in corporate governance over the next 10–15 years.

What's the bottom line when it comes to senior-level hires?

You're always known by the company that you keep. I think that you will always have difficulty trying to 'buy' an executive with a high level of reputation and a great level of skill to be the 'poster boy' for a change in image or brand of a company. That really doesn't work.

It's how you select a leader who can amplify or create a culture. It's how you enforce that culture and don't allow behaviours that don't line up with it – regardless of the short-term financial implications.

One of the things that Jack Welch said was: No matter how good the performance is, if it doesn't deliver it within the cultural mores of the organization, it doesn't matter about the results. You can't carry people who aren't living the values, regardless of their level.

It's more than words. It's actions and the enforcement of actions to make sure that your culture is reinforcing the brand that you want to create. That's why brand and talent are two sides of the same coin, particularly when you talk about the executive suite.

Brand and diversity – Beth Brooke

16

Beth Brooke is EY's Global Regulatory and Public Policy Leader. She is responsible for shaping EY's positions on public policy, engaging with regulators, policy makers, business leaders, investors and other key stakeholders around the world to address the critical issues facing the profession and global capital markets. She is also EY's global sponsor of its diversity and inclusiveness efforts and a prominent advocate in the world for the benefits of inclusive leadership and inclusive growth. Beth is regularly named by *Forbes* magazine as one of the world's 100 most powerful women.

How did you end up in your role and how did you develop your interest in diversity and inclusiveness?

Having started my career with E&Y 32 years ago in Indianapolis, Indiana, Midwest; I had been a college athlete and I was the first woman partner in Indianapolis. So I started in a very male environment. I got so much responsibility so early that gender just wasn't an issue, in part because of being in a great office, a great culture, very inclusive environment, and I was an athlete. It neutralized gender differences in a very favourable way. That was an important learning about the importance of athletics.

Then a mentor in Indianapolis sort of arranged something for me to work on in Washington, DC, and arranged at the end of the project to have it presented to the head of the tax practice. The next day, that person in head of the tax practice called me up, had me come to New York and offered me a transfer to Washington to run the national insurance tax practice. It was a direct result of a partner in Indianapolis sponsoring me to make that happen, and then getting me up to go off to Washington where I just exploded in terms of career growth. Gender just was not even on my radar screen.

I left EY a couple of years later to work in the Clinton administration, which was so diverse: you were never in a meeting that wasn't just unbelievably diverse, not just from a gender perspective but from every perspective imaginable. I got to experience first-hand every day the great innovation that resulted as a result of that. The better decision making, the better discussion, frankly, around decisions.

When I rejoined the firm a couple of years later, it was kind of a stark contrast. 'Whoa! Where'd all that diversity go?' While the firm was clearly more diverse than it had been, it was still not diverse compared to the environment I had just left. That was again a kind of a transformative moment, to see it and then see it go away, and just to see the difference in decision making and innovation that resulted.

The final thing I would say is going on the Americas board for the first time, being the lone female voice in the room and struggling to be heard, not because they didn't want to hear, but just that age-old fact that without a critical-mass voice, the minority just doesn't get heard. Yet I was on a very important body, and I needed to be heard, and couldn't figure out why I wasn't. It felt like it was all about me. I thought it was about the quality of my ideas versus the type of my gender and the minority voice.

That was a little unsettling at first until I grew into realizing my ideas were just fine. They were as fine as they always had been. I had come from a tax practice, which was really inclusive, into an environment that was a little less so.

What would be the things you have observed or learnt that companies can take to heart when they try to build diversity and inclusiveness into the way they operate?

I think many companies start by paying attention to the inherent diversity of people. Inherent meaning age, gender, race, ethnicity, sexual orientation, whatever. They try to get kind of a mix of inherent diversity, but then they don't pay attention. I think many organizations to this day are not paying enough attention to the kind of leadership that allows that inherent diversity to actually produce better decisions and produce more innovation.

The research shows that diverse teams perform either really, really well, or they're just awful. The difference is how well they're led. Even if you have a diverse team, if it's not well led, you actually not only don't get the benefit of the diversity – better decision making, better innovation – you actually get worse outcomes because it's not well led. Therefore it's not well managed. Difference and diversity is amplified instead of maximized.

Not all organizations are focused on that leadership piece, which I actually think is of the new frontier. The complex nature of business today really demands inclusive leadership now, and does demand the *inherent* diversity of perspectives.

You refer to it as inclusive leadership. What does that mean to you?

There are a lot of sensitivities that come with a leader that really is starting to get it. They're willing to take advice. They're willing to understand that, as a leader, no one today has all the answers, and that puts them in a mindset of allowing others to speak up. In fact, encouraging others to speak up. They make it safe to risk sort of dissenting ideas or novel ideas. They make that very safe. They ensure everyone gets heard. Again, sort of making sure they speak up. They share credit when there's a team success. They empower team members to make decisions.

They check their own assumptions at the door. Every leader has their own opinion. They know where they're trying to go, but a real inclusive leader is able to kind of check that at the door, recognize that the power of the group is going to bring us things that won't fit their frame of reference and may not even sound that good to them. If they listen long enough and listen to enough diversity, their own views won't necessarily adhere to that other person's views, but they'll adjust. They'll adapt. They'll take it on board and the synthesis will provide a better outcome.

When you look at the whole value chain of innovation, the minority view that's raising novel ideas often gets killed, because they're being heard by a leader who doesn't understand their frame of reference or perspective and, therefore, deems it not a great idea.

The women in our organization see tremendous economic opportunity among women as a buyer channel. But I have to tell you. It's been like pushing a rock up a mountain for years on that issue – until we named a new leader.

Suddenly we're getting traction. It's just that simple. The person in charge understands and now happens to have the same frame of reference, so now it's easy to have the novel ideas heard, but it's so interesting to have for years felt that you just had to go so far out of your way to sell an idea to the rest.

That's the epitome of people who are not inclusive leaders. They can't see the world through anything but their own lens, and they assess the worthiness of ideas through that lens.

One of the parallels is the lack of diversity when it comes to functional perspectives on problems.

Oh, absolutely. I find that all the time. Functional diversity is just as important as gender or anything else. I mean, to me, inherent diversity is by function, too.

Clearly, the same kind of techniques that a leader would use from a gender and related perspective would be exactly the same kinds of behaviours they need to take from a functional point of view then. So what stops that from happening from your point of view?

I test myself. If I walk into a room, who do I naturally gravitate to? I will gravitate to the women, because we enjoy talking with each other. If you leave me to my own devices, and I don't check myself, I'll wake up one day, and I've hired an entire team of women. Why? Because they tend to think like me. Their styles are more like me.

What people get rewarded for by and large is getting projects done fast. They've got to be good enough. Could they have been better? Well, it's hard to tell that you could have gotten a more innovative outcome or a more innovative solution, because you don't know it existed.

You just got the result that you got with a homogeneous group, and no one can sit back and say there was something better out there, because it didn't exist. I think we get by this way for years, and society thinks we're doing just fine with homogeneity, because we just don't know what we're missing, but the research shows very clearly what we're missing.

How do you get people to kind of realize the power of inclusivity and diversity in the way we are discussing it?

First, you've got to tell them the facts. Back it up with the research, which is so overwhelmingly clear.

Then, I think you've got to help them experience it. That's where the real change comes. You can have it in their heads, but it doesn't get to their heart until they experience it. Once they have experienced being on a diverse team that is well led, they'll never go back. You just see so many people today that just wouldn't do things any other way.

I know, for myself, I walk into a room and I don't even think about it, but I instantly know whether I've walked into a non-diverse room. I know I've got to go check the solution against somewhere else, because the risk of having a sub-optimal outcome is high. I do it without even thinking now, but that's my having experienced the benefits of it.

I recall talking to guys in particular, who got moved from what's comfortable to what's harder, which is to manage a diverse team, through that transition process. Once they've done it and they've gotten the benefits, then it gets so much easier each time.

I really do liken it to establishing a workout routine. You hear so many people who just want to be more fit, and they just can't make it through that first two months, where you got to get up and do it every day, even though it hurts and you don't like it, because at the end of that two months, you're going to be addicted to it. Your body's going to crave it. It's the same thing with working with a diverse team. It's not easy. It's harder at first, until it's not. Then, you'd never do it any other way.

How do you think you can try to demonstrate as a brand that you're genuinely more diverse and inclusive?

There's a variety of ways. One is the nature of your workforce, and what your workforce says about you. Do they feel valued? Do they feel empowered? I think organizations that are truly diverse and inclusive will do well on those attributes. I know one of the things to form the biggest effect of retention is an answer to the question of 'Do I feel valued? Do I feel included for my opinions?' One of the greatest predictors of retention and engagement.

How does the marketplace feel?

I think the marketplace sees it in terms of how they're served and the teams they're served with. I think they recognize it in terms of the solutions they're getting. Could they tell you that's because the organization is more diverse? I don't know about that, but they certainly favour you as an organization for the kinds of results you produce.

I think if you're a product company, it would manifest itself in the nature of your products. You think about the car companies over the years. They had no diversity in their engineering design teams. They're finally starting to wake up and realize that women are the primary purchasers of the car-buying decisions, and yet the cars are being not designed with them in mind at all.

The economic power of women outside the traditional workforce, and the power that they could have as an economic driver, is staggering. What role do you see them playing, and how do organizations make the most of that, or should they make the most of that?

Women are economically a high-growth market, emerging market, across all geographies. There will be 870 million to a billion women over the next decade coming into economic power as workers or as entrepreneurs because they now have been educated and enabled. That impact of those billion women coming into economic power over the next decade is of such size that it has an impact third in size behind the growth of India and China. It's that big of an impact.

When I talk to CEOs, I say, 'You'd never think of not investing in India. You'd never think of not investing in China. Why aren't you thinking about investing in women, given this third billion effect behind India and China? What I mean by that is, as a CEO, how are you thinking about your products? How are you thinking about what's going into them, or your services?

'Look at the makeup of your board. Look at the makeup of your senior leadership. We know that one of the great things in innovation, the reason you want a diverse set of perspectives trying to work on solutions is because they will see the needs of a market through their own lens, so if you don't have enough women in senior leadership or on your board, you are not seeing the market for this emerging market of women clearly enough.'

How do you actually get from where we are now to that more inclusive diverse level of senior leadership?

Number one, you've got to believe it. You've got to believe it matters. It can't be lip service. You have to actually believe it matters. It probably means you've experienced it for yourself, and you're a believer.

You've got to know your numbers across your organization. Know what the organization looks like. There are people not going to be where you want them to be. Then you've got to commit to how to move them. That takes a combination of sponsorship, succession planning, looking out three to five years, so that you're looking at people for what they can achieve. Everybody will look around and go, 'Ah, there's nobody qualified for these roles.' Well, okay: Look out three to five years. How are you going to get them ready so that three to five years from now, we're not saying it again in three years' time? What kind of career experiences are we going to give them? How are we investing to move people around so that they are qualified three to five years out? That's what it takes, and that's what's not happening in most organizations.

From a brand perspective what really matters?

From a brand perspective, not just internally focused, where do you invest your time and your money and your energy and your resources? If I take ourselves, for example, we're so heavily invested in advancing the economic power of women, not within our own organization, but outside, and we're so involved in so many things around that.

That affects your brand. We are known as being committed, not in a self-interested way, but in a publicly interested way in the advancement of women, because we recognize they are an emerging market. It is an enlightened self-interest in that we know they'll be our clients someday. Those are the things that really, really distinguish your brand when you actually believe and put your money and resources and time and sweat and equity into those things that are genuinely in the public interest.

17

Brand, talent and the new world of work – Dave Coplin

Dave Coplin is Chief Envisioning Officer at Microsoft UK. He is a passionate advocate of demolishing work 1.0 as we know it. His views are more fully explained in his book *Business Reimagined*.

How did you end up as 'Chief Envisioning Officer' at Microsoft UK?

It's a pretty simple story, really, in that I'm an IT guy. I have been all my career. One of the things is that I'm a forward-looking IT guy. About six or seven years ago, I started really thinking about the power of consumerization and the systemic power of consumerization, and then realized that I had no experience in the consumer side of IT.

One of the nice things when you work for a company like Microsoft is that there are always lots of opportunities around the business. For the last three years, I've been on the consumer side of our business, but still maintaining that view on the overarching role of technology in a modern society.

One of the things I've been really lucky to do with Microsoft is to pick up this platform, which is: Let's really understand the human side of the equation. Let's talk about the future of humanity. I get that's a bit over-the-top, but what does the society of the future look like? How are people going to work? Then, when we understand a bit more about that, then we can start thinking about what kind of technology we're going to need, or what kind of policies we're going to need to support that technology.

Those things can really weld together, and obviously the position at Microsoft gives me a great platform, both in terms of understanding what we think is coming, but equally, in terms of seeing how all sorts of different people use technology – whether it's our largest customers or it's the consumer stuff that we do.

You talk a lot about mindsets being rooted in outmoded models and ways of thinking. How does that play with the 'brand and talent' view of the world?

The interesting thing is that technology is only a problem in the sense that it is used by human beings. My concern is more about how humans both perceive and use technology, than it is about the limitations of the technology itself. I firmly believe the way most organizations are structured goes back a couple of hundred years. It goes back to how we formed this sort of command-and-control culture, which typically came from church and the military.

We've moved to this world from the Industrial Revolution, the Manufacturing Revolution and now the Knowledge Revolution, where that mentality has just propagated itself. Whenever we get new technology, all we tend to do is to use it to replicate what's always happened before.

My poster child example of this is e-mail. We had an analogue process called office memos, where I would go and get a piece of paper, and I would write a message, and stick it in an envelope, and send it to you. Then along comes technology, and all we do is digitize the process. We don't think about if the process is right. We don't think about if the process could be done differently. We take what we have, and we digitize it.

And in e-mail, we've made it so easy, cheap and friction-free to send that memo, that we just send more e-mails. We don't sit and debate: 'Actually there are different ways we can communicate. What would be the most appropriate way to communicate this specific message?' We've just got this tool, and we think, 'Yes, that's fine. Let's use e-mail.'

Over time, you end up in this place where productivity is the problem. The tool has taken over the role or the process as work.

Another example is people who complain about being given a mobile e-mail device. They complain about the fact that now they're expected to be on, 24/7. Whereas, the reality is, these technologies were supposed to free you, they were supposed to empower you, not imprison you.

Somewhere along the line, we've lost the plot. We've forgotten that actually our job is to find the most appropriate way for us to work as adults, the most appropriate way for us to work, the most efficient way for us to work. We've simply become slaves to what the technology allows us to do, based on what we've always done.

The interesting thing right now, and, to me, the most fundamental because of this thing called consumerization, is that we now have a really rich experience of technology in our personal lives. It isn't special or unique. It's just a normal part of everyday life.

We're now expecting to do things differently inside the workforce, and that's where the magic happens because, all of a sudden, I want to communicate differently. I want to collaborate differently. I want to think more proactively about what the technology could do for me. That's where I think the real change is going to start to happen.

There are some intriguing similarities when you compare, say, the evolution of the branding industry and the emergence of social media.

This happened in social media: If you only want to allow your consumers to engage with your brands in a way that is consistent with your brand guidelines, guess what happens? Nothing. Nobody engages with you.

If you remember the journey that we've been on, through this experiment, it's been like social media, where blogging first arrived, and most companies sent out a missive, 'Thou shalt not blog.' Because it's communication externally, it's a PR thing, we want to manage the way it goes.

Now we've got this really interesting space where people start to get comfortable with the fact that people can have their own voice. There were problem areas, especially an organization like Microsoft where you've got, on the inside, information that's not yet ready for the outside. For example, waiting on a big launch.

We changed a lot for the past few big product launches – for example Xbox 1, Windows 8. People outside of those product teams knew nothing about what was going on inside. The only way I, a Microsoft employee, could find out about Xbox 1 was sitting on the live stream with everybody else watching it being launched in Seattle.

But that's part of the way that we felt with empowering people with the brand. It's a maturity thing in an organization, and we've seen this play out with social media: being relaxed enough with the branding guidelines to allow people to tell that story in their own words, but not so relaxed that they can wander off.

It's the same thing with functional silos: you suddenly get cottage industries of people re-imaging what you want to be famous for and achieve – but in their own words. Which is not a problem as a master brand, but it can get challenging.

I probably need to point out here that since we recorded the interview, we have announced a massive reorganization of our business and structure which really intends to fix the problem I talked about here. You may just want to be mindful of that.

We've historically had this problem at Microsoft if I'm really honest. And part of this problem at Microsoft is we make so many different sub brands.

Often the master brand is forgotten, misunderstood, and not being thought about. And part of my role inside the organization is to just bring a little bit of awareness to that. And I think we've seen a massive difference in employee engagement, but also how our employees go on to become evangelists for our brand – in a constructive, non-religious way.

It's empowering people with the strength of the brand, but also helping them to channel our brand story in their own words, in their own way so long as they don't lose the core meaning. The good news is, we've just announced a major restructuring that should help mitigate this.

Taking technology out of the equation, you now have brand agencies that are serving marketing directors, and you have HR and human capital agencies that are serving the HR directors. Each creating their own ways of doing things. The fact is, that's completely nonsensical. An organization has one brand. It happens to express itself in different ways, to different audiences, in different media.

The way we interpret that and deal with that is that organizations should be oriented around common goals. What is it that your brand, your organization is here to do? Within that, the challenge is to empower every single member of the workforce to do whatever they can to help achieve that outcome.

While that sounds really big, it means that most people are organized in organizational silos, and, worse still, their jobs have become separated from the outcome of what they do, because they're focused on the standardization of processes. I'm no longer making a car. I'm making widgets, and the more widgets I can make more quickly with more quality the better my salary and my compensation, my bonus will be. Whether the car's any good or not doesn't matter to me because I'm making widgets. I think there are two really subtle but important things about that change, or that problem. Number one is if I'm not really connected to how good the car is then I've got no vested interest in using any of my skills other than widget-making in making that car better. I'm not really in touch with that outcome.

The second thing which is most important is around agility. If your organization is constructed out of functions each focused on processes, if your market fundamentally changes you can't react quickly enough to those changes because you've got to reorient your entire operating model and processes. So you can't go from making cars to aeroplanes or making cars to making cakes because you're only set up to make widgets.

The first principle is the organizational outcome, then the tactical interpretation. We get turned around sometimes, don't we?

Certainly for the UK employees, I want to create a group of passionate individuals who understand the outcome that our organization can bring. I'm not so religiously wedded to the idea that the only way they can talk about that is with a script.

It's that proper human type of advocacy that makes the difference. It shows that this is a company that listens, engages and is thoughtful.

I think you have to take these people on that journey. You have to help them understand. Some people get it right, some people intuitively get it, but what I find is, you go through cycles.

Now, the tough bit: what are the solutions?

Well, the funny thing here is a bloke from Microsoft saying that the technology has absolutely nothing to do with the solution.

It needs to be there and it needs to enable, but you don't solve this problem by having better technology or by having more technology. The analogy we sort of use is: If I stick another telephone on your desk it doesn't mean you're any better at communication or collaboration. In fact, actually, it just adds more stress and has a detrimental effect rather than an incremental effect. So the reality of this is that actually it's about how you think about the way you manage your organization, but really specifically it's about how you empower your employees.

If you take the structure, take away the hierarchy of the organization and you create this organism, rather than organization, that can adapt, that can change, that can sort of mould and weave itself to whatever the situation that you find yourself and your marketplace in. One of the best examples we have access to is Yammer.

While the tool is wonderful, what's even more wonderful from my perspective is you look at how that organization is run by its management team and what you will see is this incredible concept of leadership rather than management. For the leaders of Yammer, their entire job is getting out of the way. They want to make sure that they've empowered every single employee to meet their overall outcome as an organization. If they have to come and ask permission or if they have to get sign-off from the leadership, then the leaders have failed. That's pretty much how they do it.

There is very little in terms of hierarchy there, so anybody can ask anybody anything, and it's all an open conversation. What that does is it enables people to explore the skill sets that they can bring to that organization, not just the stuff that they were hired to do, but the stuff that they can really add value to.

This is the most challenging part of this from a managerial perspective. Effectively you have to let go of that command-and-control mentality that we've had as a society for a couple of hundred years. You have to say, 'Do you know what? I'm going to let my people do what they think is right.'

It's a bit like what Netflix does and its work culture. The two things that stand out from that for me are they have no holiday entitlement. You can take a holiday whenever you want. The second thing is that their only expenses policy is: 'Act in Netflix's best interest.'

What we see happen when you do that to people: You empower people, you say, 'We trust you to be professional about what you do with us here.' All of a sudden not only am I excited by what I can give, I become responsible for it, too. I want it to be good. I will over-deliver and over-commit because, 'Hey, these guys trust me. This is incredible.' Compare that to where we've come from, which is people micro-managing individuals where there is no discussion about how to get things done.

The difference between a leader and a manager is, when a leader gets asked to do something by their boss, a manager will take that ask and then chunk it down and allocate different tasks to members of the team. A leader will take that ask and show it to the team and say, 'Right, this is the ask. How are we going to do it?' So it's that sense of empowerment that I think really is at the core of what the organizational change brings. It provides an empowering sort of levelling effect.

I'll tell you a little personal story. The other day I'm on Yammer and there's this conversation about the fact we've run out of Bing branded sweatshirts in the company store in Seattle. Who should be on this thread, but Qil Lu. You know, this guy exists in the stratosphere of the organization, and he is answering... he's saying, 'Seriously, we've run out of sweatshirts? Hey, Adam, listen mate, can you go and sort that out? We need to get more sweatshirts.'

Now, old school we'd say 'Hasn't he got something better to do with his time?' New school, people like me look at this and say 'My God, that's incredible.' Not only is this guy into strategy, he's got all of our long-term direction. He's plumbed in to what we have to do on a day-to-day basis. And that sort of filled me with a sort of pride and confidence, and also makes me feel like I'm part of this thing, I could reach out, I could chat to this bloke if ever I thought there was an issue.

And these are all of the senses, cultural changes that this kind of collaboration brings. It fundamentally changes the way we think about the world of work.

Brand, talent and strategy – Mike Cullen

18

Mike Cullen leads EY's Global Talent Function, bringing together talent leaders from geographies and service lines to ensure EY attracts outstanding people both off campus and as experienced hires. He also empowers and develops people within the organization and connects with the many EY people now working outside the organization. He is responsible for developing and delivering EY's promise to their people *'Whenever you join, however long you stay, the exceptional EY experience will last a lifetime.'*

Following a 12-year career in financial services, Mike joined EY as a partner in the UK Financial Services Group in 1992. He has held a number of senior roles at Country, Area and Global levels including UK Head of Financial Services Advisory, UK Managing Partner – Markets, EMEIA Managing Partner – Accounts, Industries and Business Development, EMEIA Managing Partner – People and Global Managing Partner – Markets.

How did a financial services professional become global people leader at EY?

I'm actually a marketer by background. I began in financial services as the Marketing Director for an insurance company and then spent five years at Price Waterhouse before becoming the partner responsible for consulting services to the insurance industry at EY in 1992.

My first foray into what they called the 'people space', which in my point of view is the link between markets, brand and talent, and the people agenda, was in 2005. My remit later was to bring our EMEIA [Europe, Middle East,

India and Africa] Area to life in the marketplace, otherwise the formation of an Area grouping would just have been seen as a cost-reduction exercise as we integrated.

I became the Managing Partner for People and Clients which is the first time we'd ever linked the two together, which I suppose is almost synonymous with this book, *Brand and Talent*. People and Clients signalled an interesting shift, because for the first time we were bringing together the direct relationship between the people at the organization, the skills that you need and the development of sustainable client relationships based upon exceptional client service.

The ethos in the organization had to be the development of sustainable relationships. As a $20 billion business by then, we couldn't be a transaction-orientated business. You can't start a $20 billion business from zero every financial year. Therefore, it is all about the sustainability of services and the sustainability of relationships – and there is a different mix of skills and talent needed to build and sustain that type of business.

That brings us up to date with the new EVP and brand positioning for EY.

Yes. I was asked a couple of years ago to do a second tour of duty on the Global Executive, to do what we did in EMEIA but to do it globally, which is still my focus today. We are setting out on another refresh of our strategy. Having now grown from an $8.2 billion business in 2000 to approximately a $25 billion business today, we are now focusing on growing to a $50 billion business. What does this growth mean for market shift, what does it mean for the future state of the brand?

The next ten years will bring further changes and adjustments to the talent mix, but perhaps the biggest single difference will be a change in talent location. If the last ten years were about a shift in the mix of talent, the next ten years will be a fundamental shift in where you need that talent to be. Hence the fundamental changes and growth in the emerging markets, the onshore/offshore debate about where you locate some critical resources, and resource pooling in the business.

On the theme of moving from talent mix to talent location, when you look at the CEO agenda for most companies, two things come up. One is brand and the other is shortage of skills. How is the skills shortage, or the perceived shortage of the right kind of talent, affecting your growth plans and how are you trying to tackle that?

The skills shortage in fast growth markets is the big people challenge for any business looking to grow quickly in these markets. It means we have needed to rethink business models, hence the need to trigger more strategic mobility in the organization.

We currently spend more as an organization on mobility than we do on acquisitions. We are putting a lot of effort into building a mobility strategy as a strategic investment. We are constantly making sure we target the right skills to the right markets.

We are also shifting our mindset as an organization from that of an historical, Anglo-American, Western European one. We are looking at sourcing talent, for example, from the emerging markets. The major business schools in China or India are obviously churning out high calibre graduates. This forces a major shift in your talent acquisition programs in those markets.

The big challenge to a business like EY is all of the things you have to do to change the price point of your services. When the emerging markets are 10 or 12 per cent of the business, your historic, traditional price points, and cost base, have got a more Western orientation. But if you develop a plan that says, 'Over the next five to six years we believe 35 per cent of our business will be in the emerging markets', then we know they're not going to pay 'mature market prices', and therefore you've got to change your price points, which means you've got to change your cost base. So, how to change your cost of delivery? For us, in professional services, that is the explicit link back to talent hubs and where you locate the people.

You can't just keep flying in Western experts that cost Western prices because it's just not price competitive in those markets. It heightens the need for a restructuring of the business model, on where you provide those services and how you provide those services in those markets.

I wanted to move onto internal engagement and its relation to both talent acquisition and talent management and development. You've done the business linkage study: could you describe that?

You can't have change in the partnership environment without linking people's hearts and minds to their wallets. We had to get people to stop seeing the talent agenda as something different, something in a silo 'over there'. So we did what we call the Business Linkage Study to prove to a lot of financially aware partners, accountants, tax, and finance people, that there was a direct linkage.

Research shows there's a great link between talent programs, in particular engagement, and improved return on capital or performance of a business. It has never been looked at before, however, in detail in a professional services environment. It's one thing for me to recite some book, or research, from

Harvard to our partners. But then they'd say, 'But that was to do with a commercial organization, it won't work for us.'

We tried to show linkages. We do a global brand survey and a global people survey every two years, and an interim survey every year. As I'm a marketer by background, when people would say to me, 'What do you think of the global people survey?' I'd say that the results, while important for this business as a stand-alone study, need to be made more powerful by correlating it to the global brand survey. This is because the people are the brand in the market place.

The first thing we found in that Business Linkage Study was a direct correlation between the brand favourability index of all of our business units around the world, and the engagement index, which is something we measure in the global people survey. There's a fundamental linkage between what our people think of the organization, and the brand favourability index which is what our clients think of the organization.

The second thing we showed was that recruitment and retention levels in an organization like this are also linked to brand favourability. We hire a lot of people each year, and the nature of our business model means a lot of people leave each year. We recruit something like 50,000 people a year, but upwards of 40,000 people can leave every year.

Of course, retention levels are important, and we discovered a direct correlation between the engagement index of our business units around the world and their retention levels. There was a significant difference in the retention levels between our most engaged and our least engaged business units. A 1 per cent movement in retention levels can be worth $100 million to this business, in terms of what it costs to hire and recruit different people. So if you can see a significant variation between your highest and lowest engagement levels, it's huge. It's worth a lot of money to the business in terms of money, and in terms of client continuity, client service, linkages to brand, client satisfaction and so on.

Third, so I could focus on people's wallets, we found a direct correlation between the engagement levels of our people, and the revenue per head in the business, to the tune of tens of thousands of dollars per person difference between our most engaged and our least engaged business units.

It wasn't just about the cuddly people agenda – 'go be nice to your people'. It was about 'this is really impactful in the business'.

Now that you've got all of the elements in place, now it's how are you going about doing that? What are the tools, and mechanisms, and levers you're using to try to drive that engagement on?

We broke down elements of our people proposition into different components. We asked ourselves the questions 'how do you engage people before they join, when they're here, and after they leave?' This helped us build advocacy for EY as a service provider and as an employer.

That gave us a realization about what we are as a business. We are a big talent development machine. That is a good thing, not something to be ashamed of. We concluded that our employment proposition had to be one that recognized the individual's 'whole of life experience' with EY. It's the opposite of blindly assuming we offer everything to everybody and therefore people want to stay here forever.

Like any business, some people stay a long time, some a very short time.

We needed to fully understand: Why do people come here? Why do they stay? And we figured out that it's the 'whole of life' experience and value we offer. Hence our EVP that we've arrived at, 'Whenever you join, however long you stay, the exceptional experience you'll get here will last you a lifetime.' That resonated around the business. For example, when we go to campuses now, we will say 'Come to EY and develop your career at EY'. But we'll also take along with us alumni to that campus who will say, 'I came to EY, stayed five years, ten years, fifteen years, and now I'm running my own business. I'm an entrepreneur, I'm the CFO of a major corporation in Dallas.' So people could see a career at EY is a route to success not just here but also in the external market place.

Our proposition used to say that we attract future leaders for EY, but we have since changed that to say we seek to attract future leaders. Full stop. Some of those people will be the future leaders of EY, but some of them will go into politics, some will be in major corporations, some great entrepreneurs. The 2012 World Entrepreneur of the Year is an EY Alumnus.

The other thing we tried to discover was what we need to do for people when they are here. Through research we did with Susan David, a Harvard professor, we looked at some of our best in class engagement locations as well as some or our external research on engagement.

What was the pixie dust that triggered high levels of engagement around the world? There were two aspects of that. One was that people needed to feel more empowered, and therefore more in control of their own destiny. They're focused on getting things done, as opposed to being micromanaged. The other was about teaming, and a key revelation of that was that when people felt they were working on engagements that stretched them to the end of their professional capabilities – but in a supportive and rewarding teaming environment – they felt more engaged.

The linkages between empowering people to do their best, and working on stretching and stimulating work in an environment that we felt was supportive in teaming, allowed us to focus on this whole ethos – one of high performance teaming.

We've done a lot of work now, breaking down what we mean by teaming, looking at what the characteristics of high performing teams are and what are the characteristics of the leaders of high performing teams. We have developed programmes for our partners that teach them how to understand what the components are of high performing teams. How diverse are they? We know that diverse teams – led properly – deliver better results. We are shifting culture, over time, to create the environment in every office that can make that thrive.

When you talk about people engagement, what are the things you really think are important to focus on? There's this wonderful word 'engagement'. In a tangible way, what are you trying to do to increase levels of engagement so that people feel empowered, like they're part of a high performance team?

First of all there's no magic wand for a single thing you need to do, in terms of a process of engagement. It is about how you embed things into the culture of the organization, and what we did was break down engagement into almost every point of interaction.

It's become about setting up an environment of trust as opposed to an environment of control. Critical to that, in our environment, is changing the mindsets of the 9,500 partners who will run these teams. What we've tried to do now is embed it into an empowerment structure for the partners, not only in the culture, structure and philosophies of the partnership, but also into the way partners are managed and measured. You don't stand a chance of embedding an empowerment culture if your leaders don't feel that way.

Talk a little bit about the new purpose of EY, and how you think that is going to help you do all the things you've been talking about. What's the purpose of the purpose? What's the role of the purpose in helping make this happen at EY?

We have now articulated in a coherent way a reason for an organization like EY to exist that's been accepted globally, both in terms of the business and also in terms of our talent proposition.

If we were just an audit business, you could say our principal purpose was to be the custodian of the capital markets. EY, however, is now a whole broad spectrum of professional services.

Our purpose is 'building a better working world', which has resonated with our people and our clients. We are building a better working world for our clients, a better working world for our people, in the experience they get and in the communities in which our people work, and in which they serve. People say to me 'The best people agenda, the best talent agenda, is a growth agenda', to which I can now respond, 'The best growth agenda is a talent agenda', because they are two sides of the same coin.

Where and how does HR, human capital management, the nuts and bolts operational stuff, fit in?

I'd describe it as HR operations, because from payroll to terms and conditions, to holidays, to benefits, to pension, we've got to run a very efficient, effective and competitive HR operation. The HR agenda in this organization is the development and maintenance of a market competitive human resources function.

That focus is totally different to me than the people or talent agenda, which is a wide-ranging strategy that focuses on the 175,000 people that work here and the 1,000,000 brand investors in the market place. That's the people and talent agenda, which is directly linked to the brand. I personally put a lot of weight in my language about the difference between an 'HR' and a 'talent', people agenda linked to brand and presence in the market. I think too many businesses don't draw that distinction, which is what you're trying to draw out in the book.

Most HR 'best practice' is all about HR becoming more strategic, and you're saying, 'No, HR shouldn't necessarily become more strategic, it should do what it does better.' How do you manage that separation given it's probably a challenging position to many HR professionals?

I don't think it's just semantics. The business should understand the difference between a people or talent agenda and an HR function. The talent agenda shouldn't be run by the HR function. If I was giving advice to an organization, I would say, 'Don't get caught up with making HR too strategic.'

The way I explain it is to position HR as a vertical and the people and talent strategy as a lateral. I would say it's fundamentally different. It's not about the elevation of the HR function; it's about understanding the difference between an HR function, the operational HR vertical, and the strategic people lateral.

I have interviewed several people in similar circumstances who tell a similar story...

In my global executive role I talk regularly to HR teams throughout the world and they often ask a really good question: 'Why is it that the business appoints people like you, a brand guy, a marketer, as talent leader? Aren't you stifling the careers of us HR professionals?' I always say: 'No. I'm not here to do your job.'

Five per cent of my job, 10 per cent tops, is to make sure the right HR professionals are in place that can run and drive the HR function. Ninety per cent of my job is driving the people and talent agenda across the organization. I wouldn't dream of being head of HR. It's not for me to stifle the careers of HR professionals. I have fantastic HR professionals that run that vertical far better than I could ever do. I drive the talent agenda in the market place, the business linkage to the brand, and in doing so help build a better working world!

Brand in a multinational conglomerate – Mr Shriprakash Shukla

19

Mr Shukla is President – Group Strategy, Chief Brand Officer and a Member of the Group Executive Board at the US$16 billion Mahindra Group. An alumnus of the most prestigious institutions in India (BTech from IIT, BHU, Varanasi and MBA from IIM Ahmedabad), he has over 32 years of rich and varied experience in managing large projects and operations. He is widely credited with taking mobile telephony to the masses by setting up telecom infrastructure in the remotest parts of India.

During 2013, Mr Shukla oversaw and orchestrated a complete makeover of the Mahindra Group's Visual Identity (including its word mark) across its 18 businesses and a large number of operating companies, as Mahindra gears up to be among the most admired top global brands in a decade.

Recognizing his passion for the people management function, he has also been entrusted with the responsibility of being the Chairman of the Corporate Centre HR Council, and Group Management Cadre (GMC) Council. Both of these cross-function and cross-business councils aim to achieve excellence and harmony in various HR policies with respect to their domain and to supplement Group HR function in its endeavour.

He is a recipient of several awards and recognitions in his field. He is also regularly invited to speak at reputed academic and industry fora.

Mahindra is an amazing example of a masterbrand that manages to have a higher sense of purpose although it operates across 18 industries. How do you achieve that?

Let me share the Mahindra example a little. Corporate brand and employer brand – do they interact with each other, do they influence each other? Yes, they influence each other tremendously.

In the United States we have the Ivy League and there are seven colleges on the East Coast, starting with Harvard. Similarly, in India we have IITs (half a dozen of them) and IIMs. These are the Ivy Leagues of engineering schools and business schools. The moment you say you're from an IIT or IIM, immediately your market value goes up because you have to be in the 99.9th percentile, otherwise you cannot get admission. At Harvard you can get admission at the 96th percentile.

Therefore, companies rush to recruit from these institutes, because they know that the *crème de la crème* of India is there. Millions apply and a few hundred are admitted. You cannot recruit better than that. The institutes have placement committees, who decide which company will be given an interview slot on which date.

We have a concept of 'A1' companies. Simply being told that you're an A1 company means that you are recognized to be among the best companies in India. If you look at the A1 company list, you can see that the employer brand and the best company brand go hand in hand. On the list you will see TATA and Mahindra, subsidiaries of reputable multinationals like Unilever and Procter & Gamble, and consulting companies such as McKinsey and the Boston Consulting Group. When these companies put up their employment notices on the notice boards of the institutes, the placement committee decides the order of campus recruiting sessions according to the number of applications these companies receive. It is a very quantitative method: your employer brand at these top institutes is already very established.

We embarked on a mission a few years back. We were an A1 company, but we said: 'With A1 you can be still among the top 20 companies in India, how do we become among the top 10?'

We decided that while the corporate sector appreciated us as a highly profitable, well-respected, solid company with ethics and innovation, we were an old-fashioned manufacturing company as far as students are concerned – because they have been educated at top-flight institutes, they are likely to be more interested in emerging sectors of the economy, not necessarily established manufacturing companies. We decided to launch an employer branding exercise, which became the 'Mahindra War Room' contest at the top business schools of India.

Case studies from across the group are shared on the website and the students at those institutes are given access. We go to each institute, with the Group usually represented by a senior business manager and the senior HR manager, acting as a team. Typically we'll give a presentation and often this is the first time many students discover that Mahindra Group is present in 18 industries. Then we tell them about the website where they will see the case studies and we invite them to form teams of three or four students.

Teams work for several months to solve the case study or business problem. In 2013 we had 17 teams arriving in Bombay. These teams have to present the problem, the alternatives and their recommended solutions. Our CEOs sit together as a panel and select the seven best entries out of these 17. The final round is where our Chairman sits alongside the six Presidents. Out of the final seven we select the winner and the runner-up.

They get an opportunity to talk to the Chairman and all six Presidents of one of the largest conglomerates in India, and to showcase their talent. It is a tremendous morale boost. They all go back to their campuses with a wonderful experience to relate. In three or four years Mahindra's ranking improved and today we are 11th, and I believe that this year [2013] we will be in the top 10.

Now somebody will say that this is only employer branding, but it goes beyond that. We are talking about 17 top business schools which have on average 500 students each, so we are talking about a population of around 9,000 students. These 9,000 students will literally run the Indian corporate sector when they leave their institutes and start work. In five years they will be middle managers, in 15 years they will be senior managers – the opinion makers of tomorrow. But even if they did not make it to the contest, even if they could not reach the final round or reached it and did not win, they now are so much more familiar with Mahindra than they were earlier.

Now this effort actually has a side benefit in that every year 9,000 of these people go out into the corporate sector, so in 10 years there will be 100,000 people in the corporate sector who have gone through this experience and perspective – and they all now know us as a big conglomerate and they have seen how well we treat people. They have seen and understood the ethics and the high moral values which we swear by and work by. What was a well-kept secret inside the Group is now becoming a public knowledge.

What about other ways you connect brand and talent as combined?

We created a management trainee scheme, the GMC – group management cadre. It means that they all join the parent company in the first year, but after two years they have a choice to move to another sector, business or company within the group. People keep moving from one sector to another and for up to six years their careers are centrally managed. That means three tenures of two years each. After six years they can adopt a company where they will then spend a longer time.

We have been very successful with this concept and actually our employer branding ranking has gone up further, because why do young graduates change jobs? While money is definitely a reason, more importantly they get bored in their first job. They start saying that I'm doing the same thing repetitively or they say I have stopped learning. This is often their biggest complaint: 'I have stopped learning, I'm not doing anything new any more.'

By creating a group management cadre, they can actually go from tractor motorcycles to retail and then to mother-care, child-care products. From there they can go to IT services and they may get posted anywhere in the world on client sites in the IT sector. They could actually be working with AT&T or Horizon Telecom, helping in the production of value added services.

That immediately changes their perspective and creates stability for them. Their whole perspective of the brand changes and even when they talk to the outside world... we have 160,000 employees, so now 160,000 employees are talking every day to at least 10 people who are outside the group. That is 1.6 million people being contacted on a daily basis by the people working in our group, 1.6 million a day. If these people have a good experience, they speak well of our group and 1.6 million people every day get positive reinforcement about Mahindra.

My best ambassador is my employee. Customers of course are ambassadors, but customers don't always share good experiences.

Do you have a core set of messages, themes or values that you use across the entire group? On the one hand there is what they actually do and say every day, but do you try to create some kind of core idea that they need to align around?

We have something called House of Mahindra. It has a foundation, our core values. There are three pillars – we call them 'Rise' pillars – and then it has a roof which we call our core Purpose. These are the three things which bind the group.

The three Rise pillars are: alternative thinking, accepting no limits, and positive impact. These are the three things we do in whatever we choose to do: we apply these tests at all times. We undertake activities which have a positive impact on society and which society needs at that moment in time.

It's well documented that the growth of our group actually reflects the growth of the Indian economy. When India needed transport and infrastructure we went into manufacturing jeeps and sports vehicles, multi-utility vehicles, but not cars – we said that India needed other things more. When India began to follow its path of green revolution because there were widespread food shortages and we had to import a lot of food grain, we went into tractors, farm implements and insecticides. Then when India embarked on computerization we went into IT.

When the process of liberalization started, the number of middle-income families starting growing and suddenly there was a large middle class with disposable income. Towards the end of the mid-20th century we had an even bigger middle class, so then we started entering businesses which cater to the middle class, for example real estate, building apartments, building resorts – today we are India's largest holiday resorts company. In the 21st century we went into 21st-century businesses: solar energy and renewable energy are today's necessities.

People have seen that these big industries will contribute to the needs of society. It is a good business strategy: you're leveraging the needs of society to create a business. They go hand in hand; they are not adversaries.

Your core purpose is?

If you sum it up in one line, it is to improve the lives of, and make a positive impact on, every stakeholder who interacts with us.

Sometimes people think of customers and neglect their employees; in our view that is not a positive way to do business. If you look after customers and exploit employees, that cannot be a positive way to do business. Some people will look after both customers and employees, but they really squeeze their vendors. That is not a good way to do business.

A large corporation cannot set such an example, because if you squeeze your vendors you're forcing them to squeeze their employees and their vendors... it is a chain. You squeeze your vendors and then they have to do the same down the line to survive, and that is a negative impact which will cascade through society.

How has globalization affected your efforts?

Someone in rural Britain or the rural United States might not know much about India or China, but someone in New York City or London will know. It is the same in India.

We decided that we needed to engage with the world more productively; while we did thousands of things, I'm confining my response to the purpose of employer branding.

We selected seven Ivy League colleges. We said that every year we will select one student from each of them in a global recruitment programme.

We recruit only non-Indians. They come to India for two years and it is compulsory that they work in India for two years, even though we have operations worldwide. When a Chinese person from New York is working in our tractor business, the Chinese person is saying 'but there could be this alternative way of doing things...'. These are the people who teach us a lot through their interaction, unknowingly, bringing their different perspective to us.

I'm sure you're aware of the research about diversity and how diverse teams can actually outperform homogeneous teams in decision making...

There is no shortage of engineers in India, so we make sure that the majority of the people we recruit are from a humanities background, because they bring a different perspective. We are strong believers in ensuring left-brain/right-brain balance.

Some companies become totally engineering driven, and some become totally sales marketing driven. But we need a balance of the two. Here we go out of our way to ensure that we achieve it.

How did you bring this all together with your branding efforts?

We did research on our word mark, which had been in existence for 12 years. We found that it was considered solid, reliable, trustworthy, warm, high quality. They were good attributes. Many companies would love to have five such attributes, and we were very happy.

But these attributes are due to our manufacturing background. When you want to enter the IT sector, or financial services, or you are in hi-tech, how do you bring in that element of hi-tech to the five solid attributes which you already have?

It took us all of 2012 to come up with a new word mark, and when we introduced it the research indicated we had added two more attributes. People now also say hi-tech and modern. We managed to add two more, hi-tech and modern, because our business composition has changed.

We thought that a new word mark would be useful because ultimately your word mark is like your signature; very often people form a view about you based on your signature. That is true as much as for external customers as for internal employees. You will see that it helped in reinforcing a new image of the company, not only for the outside world, but internally employees got excited about the new Mahindra.

Without saying we created the new Mahindra by simply changing the word mark, our people got a feeling of being refreshed. But beyond the word mark is this idea of Rise.

Tell me a little bit about Rise. You decided to go with a tag line of 'Rise' and that's quite interesting.

In 2011 we incorporated Rise along with Mahindra. We always had a core purpose and we always had our core values. Core values were the foundation and core purpose was the roof. We said now that Rise is what connects them. Rise is not an advertising slogan, Rise is not an advertising gimmick, it is our way of doing business, it is our business credo, it is our philosophy of doing business. We have just given it a name, but that's it. Everything we do has Rise embodied in it. Rise of the individual, Rise of the society, Rise of every stakeholder, everybody that will benefit positively from their association with Mahindra.

It is also interesting that you are not an HR person by background, but you lead the Corporate Centre HR Council.

We decided to have a marketing person head it. This nomination came within the Group Executive Council and our President of Group HR himself endorsed that these two councils should be headed by a marketer. He thought I would bring some branding expertise to it, as well as passion: you don't have to be from HR to do HR.

People are the biggest asset of an organization; the organization may believe that it has to invest in machines, it has to invest in buildings and land, but people are first and foremost. They will create the brand.

Brand will not be created by buildings or by shining plant and machinery. On that there can be absolutely no ambiguity, ever.

20 Brand and purpose – Michael Sneed

Michael Sneed heads Global Corporate Affairs for Johnson & Johnson, covering 275 operating companies in more than 60 countries with 128,000 people. Johnson & Johnson is one of only a handful of companies that have flourished through more than a century of change.

The company is renowned for its decentralized operating model as much as for its long-standing adherence to a way of working enshrined in the Johnson & Johnson 'Credo'. Robert Wood Johnson, chairman from 1932 to 1963, crafted the credo himself in 1943, long before anyone had ever heard the term 'corporate social responsibility'.

You've spent your entire career with Johnson & Johnson and have moved across numerous companies, divisions and geographies. It must give you deep insight into how you manage to maintain a brand and reputation across such a diverse range of people, products, services and sectors.

I always tell people I may be very biased because my entire career has been with Johnson & Johnson. I started off in the marketing organization and progressed to our OTC healthcare company. I did a stint in business development and then ran our international OTC business for about three years. From there, I moved into general management and managed our nutritional business first in Europe then globally. I came back to the United States and oversaw the North American Consumer business and then I moved over to our medical device sector, and for five years I ran our Global Vision Care business.

I've been here on the corporate side overseeing what's called Global Corporate Affairs, which is really a portfolio of several enterprise-wide functions such as Communications, Global Marketing, Corporate Equity and Philanthropy. So, I have a pretty good feel for the product marketing side and the brand marketing side along with what we like to say is the corporate 'trust mark', so really the corporate brand versus the product brand.

What are the biggest barriers and challenges between making sure you get the corporate trust mark built, established and protected in the marketplace, and its overlap with your desire to put together a compelling and differentiated talent brand?

I actually don't think there's a conflict, especially when it comes to J&J. Part of that starts with the fact that from a corporate culture perspective we always tend to lead with our values and our value statement. That really permeates everything we do; it shows up differently depending on the audience or the stakeholder, but they are very much in sync with each other.

When I think about the development of a corporate brand, there are two pieces. Probably 80 per cent of it is really around this issue of 'reputation'. Reputation is about everything you do. It can't be managed, and people who think they can manage reputation are working on the wrong things.

Reputation is the summation of a lot of individual acts over a long period of time and the entity or corporation develops that reputation.

Then there is the remaining 20 per cent, which I would say is truly equity building or brand building, and that piece can be managed. That's the proactive part of your brand equity and you can extend that and make sure it is in the external market through advertising, through the media, through various stakeholders. It's the story that you want to tell.

But, again, at least for me, I am always careful to understand that that only goes so far, and it helps you be part of the conversation, which is important in this environment. But it doesn't, and it is not designed to, paper over all the other things that happen on the reputation side, which are driven behaviourally.

Now when you take a look at how does that square with a recruiting brand or your people, it's very much a reflection of the values that we express. And whether that's got a piece of equity advertising or if it's a piece of recruiting material, it starts in the same place for us. My group works extremely well recruiting people because all the material that we develop on the corporate brand side is actually used for recruiting as well. So they are in sync with what the corporate brand is; they recognize that there's little value in creating different positioning or different employer sub brands that are not in sync with where the parent or the corporate brand wants to go. I've never looked at the two as really being at odds with each other.

How do you articulate and how do you try to engage your people, and candidates, in those values and in the Credo on a day-to-day basis?

That is clearly the focus. We talk about return engagement, which is a metric that I'm not sure a lot of folks talk about, but I think more and more companies will be doing so in the future.

So, if you want to maximize engagement, which is what a lot of companies want to do in the space with their employees in particular: what is the strategy around it, what is the focus, and then what is the specific plan? With Johnson & Johnson, we've always thought very highly of our employees, of course, as every company does, but what I have challenged our folks to do is two things.

First and foremost, think of your employees as another group of key stakeholders just like we think of our investors, just like we think of our customers, our consumers, our patients and doctors. They are stakeholders and they need to be talked to and they need to be part of the conversation.

Secondly, let's think of them as *the* most important stakeholders that we have, because interestingly the multiplier effect of having an engaged stakeholder, known as your employee, is tremendous relative to other stakeholders.

The first thing is to adopt the mindset that you're going to treat your employees as a key stakeholder group. Then, you're going to actually build an organization that's 100 per cent dedicated to continuous engagement with that stakeholder. That's what we try to do at J&J: One, have that mindset and Two, we built an organization called strategic communication for lack of a fancy title. That group is 100 per cent dedicated to engaging with our employees as stakeholders every single day. And the great thing about this group is they have the ability to use all of the tools that are necessary to do that in many different ways. I go back to my marketing days, and in marketing you need to tell your story more than once. You've got to keep telling it. You have to figure out how to tell it in different and creative ways, and you have to use all the channels that are available to you.

With employees it's no different: you have to be able to do all those things. The last thing that we try to really focus on is: if you believe that your employees are a stakeholder, if you believe they're one of the most important stakeholders, then you have to make sure you give them the tools so that they can actually be ambassadors for the company.

That's been the biggest change for us – not only are we talking to them and providing them with all the kind of information that you would expect of any company, but more and more we're actually giving them the tools to be able to go out and become ambassadors for the company and ambassadors for the brand. And I think that's been something that they've wanted to do and wanted from the company – but that we were tone deaf on this issue until now.

We didn't really understand what that means or what that meant. Now we do and we actually provide our people with the ability to tweet about Johnson & Johnson. We provide them with the ability to actually have presentations that they, if they're involved in various clubs and organizations, can use to go and talk about the company. We try to make it as easy as possible for them to do that. We have a resource set up for employees to just go and get information about various topics within the organization.

We try and make it as easy as we can so they can be ambassadors. So, I think it's those three things that we probably do today that we didn't do as late as 18 months ago.

Have you seen a significant change because of that?

That's the good news: we have we've seen a real uptake in the level of engagement. We just did a pulse survey and in the year-end data it was up significantly from the year before. So, 2012 was up significantly from 2011 and we're certainly looking for that same type of increase this year.

Many organizations end up with all kinds of convoluted messages around vision, mission, values and then suddenly you get a marketing initiative. How do you handle that kind of air traffic control and 'noise management'?

You're absolutely right, and what makes it even more difficult with a company like J&J is that we are a very decentralized company. We operate over 275 different companies around the world and if you're an employee you get inundated in all the messages, and at some point it's just noise. As someone who worked with a lot of the operating companies I can tell you that was the case. We recognize that – and the other cultural reality at J&J is that it is very much of a 'bottom-up' type of organization.

So we were very reluctant to ever dictate anything from the top, because one, we often were probably going to be wrong, and two, a lot of the companies don't listen to us anyway.

We're very reluctant to ever make commandments or ultimatums. So, we did a couple of things. One, we actually reached out to our top leaders to understand what they needed from corporate.

And it was actually our leaders who said, 'Look, we need some sort of overarching framework because it will actually help us be more efficient in terms of where we want to put our resources, and what are the messages that we want to deliver.'

We were hearing that, for them, the world had become so complicated that they recognized that they weren't being as efficient, and more importantly as effective as they could be. That opened the door for us to not be *prescriptive*, but to provide a *framework* of how we wanted to portray the business, the set of values we wanted to portray and the kind of language that we wanted to use. We said, 'Look, we think these are universal to J&J, no matter where you are in the business or in the function. We think that they are strategic in the way they need to be and they also provide enough room for you to be able to adjust if you need to, but it needs to be done in this framework.'

Out of that came a corporate strategic narrative – for the first time. And that narrative really sets out in a fair amount of detail what our aspirations are as an enterprise.

Everything starts with our Credo, so our Credo is always on top.

Then secondly, what are our aspirations?

Third, what are our strategic principles? How would we like to manage the organization in the enterprise for the long term?

But then we went one step further which we've never done, which is say, 'What are the growth drivers for us?' This is what gets the organization's attention because every organization is about growth. There are four growth drivers that we want you as leaders, as companies, as functions, to focus on.

That provided a lot of clarity for people. We started getting feedback that this really helped our leaders.

No matter where you are in the organization, they were actually using the language that we proposed, and the lens by which they were looking at their businesses was through these growth drivers. They clearly voted with their time and their effort and said, 'Yes, this makes a lot of sense.' It was a very nice kind of confluence of events that made them feel much better and much more connected, quite honestly, to the overall enterprise. It's given them a framework to be able to make the kind of choices and decisions that they need to make in their individual operating companies.

It's only about a year or so old, and like anything it's the kind of thing where you have to keep doing it and doing it. And it is something that, importantly, starts with our CEO.

Every meeting we have he starts with our strategic narrative and the framework. And he does that time and time again until people recognize 'this is how we talk about the business', and I think people get more and more comfortable with doing that. And then, it just can't come from the CEO, it has to come from the management committee, and the business heads, and that's the process that continues to be ongoing. But more and more you see the organization really aligning around the narrative; they've really bought into it. It's not just a check the box, it's really how we run the business. And it's become quite effective.

The market and the world has become so dynamic and so complex that people are actually crying out for a bit of guidance and simplicity. Are there any sorts of risk with trying to take that kind of top-down approach in an organization like J&J?

Absolutely, huge risk. I'll give you two big risks. One is that we go too far and we become too prescriptive, and that's very dangerous because we sit here in New Jersey and all of our business is not conducted in New Jersey. We run the risk of really not being connected to our customers, and to our consumers, and to our patients – we get enamoured with the development and crafting of a message or a strategy that really has no place in the real world. This is the first step and I'm sure we will step back and think about are we where we'd like to be, and be careful not to go any further.

The other risk is from a reputation perspective. One of the great things about Johnson & Johnson is that as a brand it is well-known, it is a trusted brand, it's great in many ways. Historically, we have been very careful to make sure that we protect that brand and inoculate it, if you will, from other things that might be going on in businesses that are owned by Johnson & Johnson. So, when something not-so-great happens in one of our operating companies, because of the way you set up legal entities, those difficulties tend to either stay very local or at least stay within the company itself, within the operating company.

Very rarely did it ever ladder up to the corporate parent. In a world where we are trying to assert our corporate brand in a much greater way because we think it's important, the risk is that when you have difficulties, those difficulties ladder up much more quickly to the corporate parent. So, while there's great benefit if you're doing wonderful things in the marketplace and you're driving growth and you're making real headway, when a company like J&J stumbles, you're much more apt to have that reflect negatively on the corporate parent as opposed to just the individual operating company. That's one of the things that we wrestle with and we continue to wrestle with it today. And I don't know if we have a good answer yet. But, we will keep pushing ourselves to ask the tough questions and ultimately get to a solution that works for J&J.

Brand and talent – Mark Weinberger

Mark Weinberger became the Global Chairman and Chief Executive Officer of Professional Services Organization EY in July 2013. Weinberger has been a member of the Global Executive, EY's highest management body, since 2008.

EY employs more than 175,000 people globally. Mark and the other members of the Global Executive recently engaged with the organization to refresh its Purpose, Ambition, Strategy and Positioning under 'Vision 2020'.

Mark began his career with EY in 1987 in their US National Tax Practice. After several years with EY, he turned his attention to the public sector, accepting a position as the Chief Tax and Budget Counsel for Senator John C Danforth (R-Missouri). He was subsequently appointed Chief of Staff of US President Bill Clinton's Bipartisan Commission on Entitlement and Tax Reform in 1994. Under President Clinton, Weinberger also served on the US Social Security Advisory Board. In these roles he cultivated a deeper interest in large budget issues, taxes and entitlements, and developed a reputation as one of the country's leading authorities on tax policy.

In 1996, Weinberger co-founded Washington Counsel PC, a Washington DC-based law and legislative advisory firm, which merged into EY and now operates as Washington Council EY. Subsequently Weinberger became the head of EY's US National Tax Practice.

Mark returned to public service in 2001 when he was appointed by President George W Bush as Assistant Secretary (Tax Policy) of the US Treasury before once again re-joining EY in 2003.

What is most important to you as a CEO when it comes to your people and your talent agenda? What are the big challenges you face and what do you think the opportunities are?

Our business is all about people, because what we provide for our clients are the skills, knowledge and integrity of our people. So at EY we spend a lot of our time thinking about how we attract great people, how we develop them – building their skills and their knowledge – and how we put people together into high-performing teams. The teamwork aspect is hugely important, because our clients come to us with incredibly complex challenges that no individual is going to be able to crack alone. The best solutions come about through combining the right people, who can look at those challenges from lots of different angles. Promoting that is about culture; we work hard to create an inclusive culture that really helps our diverse mix of people bring out the best in each other.

With challenges, a big one for us goes back to the nature of our business. We're an organization where all of our assets get up and go home at the end of the day. We have to be the place that they want to get up and come back to the next morning, because with the calibre of people we hire, well, they don't have any difficulties going and getting jobs somewhere else. So we work hard to engage and inspire our people. That was a big part of our motivation for committing our purpose of *Building a better working world* to paper and making it EY's tagline. It's incredibly important for people to understand that what they do is far-reaching and important.

We also do all we can to ensure that the time our people spend here is really valuable to them in terms of what they learn, in terms of the experience they get and in terms of building their own personal brand. That's especially important to our young people – and the average age of an EY person around the globe is about 28 – so we're a young organization in that sense.

In terms of opportunities, when we get everything right with our people they become even more valuable to our clients. And, even if they eventually leave us, we have created advocates – ambassadors for EY. Our alumni, and we have close to a million of them around the world, go on to do great things. Sometimes they even come back to work with us again, bringing their outside experience with them. I'm a prime example – I've left EY three times, and joined four.

Yes, that speaks to your employer value proposition, which I think is unique in that it openly acknowledges that there will come a day when people want to leave EY. It's 'Whenever you join, however long you stay, the exceptional EY experience will last you a lifetime'. How did you come up with that?

We discussed that for a long time and it was less about coming up with it than acknowledging some realities about our business, the kind of people we want to work here and the way the world of work is changing.

From the standpoint of people and talent, EY is one of the world's great development machines – for lack of a better word. So we've started to think about our value proposition to our people in those terms. If you come to EY, your professional and personal brand will be polished. It will be better off than if you didn't work here. We'll give you the chance to work with the biggest and best companies in the world; we'll give you great training and great mentors.

When you leave, and become one of our 1 million alumni, serving in industry, government or academia, we want you to be an ambassador for the EY family, and will be performing your new role better because of your EY experience.

I believe that young people today – and maybe always – choose to work for organizations because they're going to be better for the experience, both professionally and personally. Further than that, they want to contribute to society and they want to work for an organization that has a purpose that they believe in.

Regarding young people's interest in contributing to the world, you also talked about EY's purpose – could you expand on that? What is it about having a purpose that is so important to you as a leader when it comes to that attraction and retention and motivation?

The people who come to work for us are an incredibly diverse group, but they tend to share some important traits – they're curious, they're intellectually hungry, they want to understand the big picture as well as the fine detail and to see everything in context. So when we talk about what EY does, well, at one level we offer services to our clients – we audit companies, we help them with their taxes, we help them with transactions, we help them improve their performance. Then there's what we do with our people, in terms of training them and so on. And there's what we do, individually and together, to help our communities. And all that's great, and it covers the 'what' of what we do day to day. But it doesn't get into the 'why' – the reasons we do what we do.

As we worked to create Vision 2020, though, it became clear that EY's purpose, although we'd never written it down, was always there. We've always had a strong sense of obligation to serve, and people count on us to deliver quality and excellence in everything we do. If you step back and look at everything we do, for clients, for each other, for our communities, it really all comes back to the idea of building a better working world. It provides the why for what we do and in a really positive, inspiring way. Because our people not only want to know the context, but also they want to feel that they're contributing to something good.

Every day, every EY person is part of building a better working world – for their clients, their families, their communities and themselves. We believe that everything they do – every audit, every tax return, every advisory opportunity, every interaction with a client or colleague – should make the working world better than it was before.

It's a simple idea, but it's a powerful one – it can start really small. We're getting great feedback from our people and our clients about it. When you provide that kind of context, it can act as a great motivator. When you're stuck in the office late at night working on a project, it's easier to do when you can think of that bigger picture.

What's your view on having a more inspirational purpose that really talks about more of the enlightened self-interest view of the world as opposed to a more hard-edged business view?

I'd agree with you that our purpose is inspirational, and that's important. The people who work for us do really want to do good as well as helping their clients and as well as earning a living.

Our purpose is incredibly important, but it's not everything. We have ambition, too, and that's where a harder edge comes into play. Having purpose gives us energy. Being clear about our ambition helps turn that energy into results. Our purpose defines why we exist as an organization, and our ambition sets out what we want to achieve. The two are intertwined: achieving our ambition helps us to fulfill our purpose, and purpose contextualizes ambition.

Our ambition is to be a US$50 billion distinctive professional services organization by 2020, with the best brand, a #1 or #2 market share in our chosen services, leading growth and competitive earnings, strong relationships with our stakeholders and being viewed as the most favored employer.

Now that you've become Chairman and CEO, what kind of insights can you share about the role? How important and how difficult it is to align a leadership team and align a business around a purpose?

I'm still fairly new to the job, so it's perhaps a bit early for me to try to offer too many lessons learned yet. But I'll start my answer generally and then I'll get a bit more specific. First, I'd say that you've chosen the right word in terms of alignment. EY is made up of 175,000 smart, talented people, so I think that leadership here is largely about getting them moving in the same direction and then letting them figure things out – because they'll come up with the right answers.

Second, the teamwork we need in terms of helping our clients tackle their challenges is just as important when it comes to managing our business. I know I don't have all the answers – but I know that I've got a great leadership team and that together we will come up with the right solutions.

Talking specifically about aligning EY around our purpose, I'd have to say that sometimes an idea is strong enough that all you have do to is get it out there and people rush to align themselves around it. Building a better working world is like that – it's so true to EY that people had picked it up and started running with before we even officially announced it. So I guess I'd say in this case that while it's important that people align around our purpose, for a lot of the reasons we've spoken about already, in this instance we've been lucky and it hasn't been difficult at all. I think my role, and the role of my leadership team, has just been to offer a bit of guidance – in a big, global organization like EY, you just want to help make sure that we're talking about the same thing everywhere.

How would you describe how brand management and talent management interact?

Look, for EY, our people really are our brand – it's not that 'brand management' and 'talent management' interact – honestly, for us, they're really one thing. Our 175,000 people and our over 1 million alumni are our brand ambassadors. They are what our clients, communities and the broader world see when they experience EY. Our people define us.

GLOSSARY

ambition   A statement that describes where the business is going, what it is trying to achieve.

brand   The sum total of what other people think, feel and believe about your organization.

brand architecture   The presentation of the way in which brands within a company's portfolio are related to, and differentiated from, one another (which helps stakeholders navigate the company offering). It relates to naming of products and services as well as sponsorships and other related communication activity/processes both internally and externally.

brand attributes   The desired words that people outside the organization would (or should) use to describe the organization.

brand engagement   Broadly, how connected people feel to your brand. Brand engagement is about how well your employees and other stakeholders are connected to, and prepared to go the extra mile for and advocate (or forgive), your products and services.

brand equity   A measure, financial or otherwise, of the value of your brand and its marketplace presence and preference.

brand identity   The visible way in which a brand presents itself to its stakeholders, including name, logo, design, colour and language, which, together, is distinctive and ownable.

customer engagement   The level of customer enthusiasm and active support and advocacy for the brand/organization.

customer value proposition   A statement that defines the point of competitive advantage of the brand, physically and emotionally – what makes it distinctive and special in the minds of customers (also known as Customer or External Brand proposition) and can be succinctly expressed as its 'Differentiator' or its 'Positioning'.

employee engagement   The level of employee enthusiasm, motivation and advocacy about their work, driven by the degree of positive or negative emotional attachment to their job, colleagues and organization. Broadly, how much people care about, and are willing to go the extra mile for, advocate (or forgive) their company, their colleagues, their communities and their customers.

employer value proposition   A statement that defines what makes the organization a desirable place to work and what differentiates it from other organizations – it clarifies the 'give and get' of the employment deal.

It performs best when it is seamlessly connected to the employee experience before, during and after their association with the organization.

internal communication   As a verb, the act of ensuring that every employee can get the information they need, the connections to other people they need to interact with, and engage in the two-way conversations they require, to deliver exceptional results in a way that is efficient and effective; and the discipline of the organization to impart business-critical information to the right employees in the right way at the right time. As a noun (internal communications), it refers to the 'stuff' that is created to make this happen. When done well, internal communication should be indistinguishable from employee engagement.

marketing/marketing management   The art and science of shaping the marketplace to maximize the ability of an organization to thrive by influencing the level, timing and composition of customer demand and ensuring the provision of relevant, valued services aligned to the brand. It should be instrumental in the development and management of product, price, position, promotion and place in the product/service portfolio.

marketing communications   The discipline within marketing and marketing management of creating mediated messages and experiences to support Marketing objectives across the relevant channels on and offline.

purpose   A statement that explains why the business exists and what market(s) it operates in. It should make clear why the world would be poorer for its absence.

strategy   A set of defined key areas of activity that the organization will focus on delivering in order to achieve its purpose and ambition. Defined, measurable objectives (KPIs) and implementation action plans flow from the strategy.

values   A set of words that define the desired working style of the organization that governs the acceptable and unacceptable behaviour of individuals working there.

TALENT MANAGEMENT TERMS

Attraction   Getting the right people to want to come to work for you and not your competitors.

Brand engagement   Broadly, how connected people feel to your brand. In this context, brand engagement is about how well your employees and other stakeholders are connected to, and prepared to go the extra mile for, your products and services.

Employer brand   Your reputation as an employer among potential and existing employees and other stakeholders. Again, it's what they say it is, not what you say it is.

Employee journey   Whether it's broken down into 2 stages or 12, there is a well-embedded concept that breaks down the experience into touch points. In broad terms, thinking through how your engagement effort applies to people at each of the following stages of the employee journey can provide great insight into who needs to be involved, the potential ROI and benefits to the business, the best media and engagement techniques to apply, and what other actions need to be taken:

- **Brand** – A person knows something about your organization, or learns about it, through a variety of touch points. These may include your consumer/corporate brand, product and service experience, word of mouth, recruitment advertising, or online experience.

- **Employer brand** – At some stage, the person considers your organization as a place where they might like to work. They seek information about your organization – again from a range of sources, most of which your organization has no control over whatsoever.

- **Attraction and recruitment** – The person decides to find out more about you, and to seek a job offer from your organization. They experience your attraction and recruitment process and decide to join you or not join you.

- **Onboarding and induction** – The person is inducted into the organization and experiences 'onboarding'.

- **First 90 days** – The person experiences their initial time with your organization, including initial perceptions, setting of initial goals, objectives and expectations, and forms a picture as to whether what you offered is what they receive.

- **Engagement** – The person continues to develop in their role (or not), and at various stages, they consider looking for a different role or challenge – with your organization or with another organization. Or, the organization considers finding a different role for the person with itself or another organization!

- **Departure experience** – The person leaves employment with your organization – and may (or may not) consider rejoining at another stage, continuing to advocate your organization as an employer, and its products and services.

Engagement   Employee engagement is broadly how much people care about, and are willing to do something extra for, their career, their company, their colleagues, their communities and their customers. When it's working well, therefore, employee engagement is a good thing for everyone on your stakeholder list. Employee engagement delivers:

- commercial and cultural benefits to the organization; and

- personal and professional benefits to the stakeholders involved.

Insanity – Doing the same thing but expecting different results. Often prevalent in branding and in employee communications. Alternatively, 'If you always do what you've always done, you'll always get what you've always got!'

ROI – Return on Investment (or Return on Involvement)   Getting more out than you would if you put your money in the bank or invested in something else (or if you want to calculate it, let us know your current discount rate):

1 *Engagement builds shareholder value.* Smart companies understand that how they attract, engage and retain their people has as much impact on their business performance as their R&D, products and services, and marketing communications. Companies that do it well outperform those who don't.

2 *Engagement builds brand equity.* Your brand and intangible assets represent something between 40 per cent and 70 per cent of the total value of your organization on your finance director's balance sheet. People make or break your reputation. And people are your greatest asset (according to your annual report). So it makes sense to manage

your reputation, as a business and as an employer, like the important financial asset it is. External brand building in the employment space is no longer just about recruitment marketing and advertising, either. It's just as much about marketing, advertising, PR, HR and internal communications.

3 *Engagement enhances productivity.* There are always going to be employees who go the extra mile, and those who don't. The trick is to have as many of the good ones as possible. People don't join a company with the intention of 'not being engaged'. If you invest in making sure that people have the awareness, attitude and tools to contribute, they will be more productive. They will contribute more, and the good ones will stay longer. Make sure that your employer brand, employer value proposition – whatever you want to call it – is working hard as a business asset. It's critical to ensuring that you get the right people, that they get productive quickly, and that you don't have to go through the process of hiring them all over again.

4 *Engagement improves talent attraction and retention.* The simple act of making the effort to engage and give people a voice is often enough to make a difference, even to cynics. What's more is that your employees can act as a key channel to market for your reputation as a business and as an employer. It's not just about being nice – it's about cost saving and improved productivity. You can reduce recruitment advertising costs as well as agency fees if people become employer brand ambassadors.

5 *Engagement affects customer attraction and retention.* Organizations invest heavily in their infrastructures, in developing products and services, in sales and marketing, in supply chain and getting their products and services to markets at the price that will yield them the most profit. The problem is, you can get all of that right – and still lose customers and market share. The truth is that for nearly all products and services, even if your performance and pricing are perfect, poor service and interaction with your people – sales forces, procurement people, customer-facing, client-facing and service staff – is where your reputation is made or broken. Customers are willing to forgive a lot if your people treat them well.

Stakeholders Depending on your objectives, your stakeholders may not be limited to employees of your organization. Often, engagement efforts need to take into account other stakeholders who may be affected by changes in the way people inside your organization think and behave.

These can include:

Your organization

- senior executives and leaders;
- business and people managers;
- employees (and their families and friends);
- contractors (and their families and friends);
- former employees;
- future (potential) employees.

Other organizations

- outsourced functions (HR, IT, etc);
- suppliers;
- partners;
- regulators and government and related bodies.

The broader community

- the investment community;
- shareholders/investors;
- environmental and corporate responsibility interests.

Your customers/consumers or clients

- potential customers or clients;
- current customers or clients;
- past customers or clients.

Your competitors

- direct 'traditional' business competitors;
- non-traditional and indirect competitors;
- competitors for talent.

RESOURCES AND
SUGGESTED READING

Aaker, D (2012 [accessed 11 October 2013]) How Red Bull Creates
Brand Buzz, *Harvard Business Review Blogs* [Online]
http://blogs.hbr.org/2012/12/how-red-bull-creates-brand-buzz/

Aaker, D (2013 [accessed 11 October 2013]) Dove: The Most
Impressive Brand Builder in the Last 15 Years?, *Prophet* [Online]
http://www.prophet.com/blog/aakeronbrands/138-dove

AccuraCast (2012 [accessed 11 October 2013]) LG: LG 1 Million Video
Views, *Somesso* [Online] http://www.somesso.com/casestudies/
lg-1-million-video-views

Antonitto, J (2013 [accessed 11 October 2013]) Power to the People:
How Kickstarter is becoming a business tool for entrepreneurs,
Bl!p, The Martino Flynn Blog [Online] http://www.martinoflynn.com/
blog/2013/05/17/power-to-the-people-how-kickstarter-is-becoming-
a-business-tool-for-entrepreneurs/

Aon Plc (2013 [accessed 11 October 2013]) *2013 Trends in Global
Employee Engagement, Consulting Performance, Reward & Talent*
[Online] http://www.aon.com/human-capital-consulting/thought-
leadership/talent_mgmt/2013_Trends_in_Global_Employee_
Engagement.jsp

Arratia, R (2012 [accessed 11 October 2013]) Just the Facts Guide: How to
choose the most sustainable products and what to ask the manufacturers,
InterfaceFLOR [Online] http://www.interfaceflor.co.uk/webapp/wcs/
stores/media/Just_the_facts_FINAL_24April2012mb.pdf

Axsium & Empathica (2012 [accessed 11 October 2013]) Focusing
Your Workforce on the Moment of Truth, *Axsium Group Inc* [Online]
http://cem.empathica.com/web-wp-workforce-management

Best Companies (2013 [accessed 11 October 2013]) Sunday Times List 2013
– 25 Best Big Companies [Online] http://www.bestcompanies.co.uk

Bi Worldwide (2012 [accessed 11 October 2013]) Mobile-Based Rewards,
Bi Worldwide [Online] http://www.biworldwide.com/en/employee-
engagement/mobile-engagement1/mobile-based-rewards

Biersma Creative (2012 [accessed 11 October 2013]) Employee
Engagement via Social Media Can Improve Retention, *Biersma Creative*
[Online] http://www.biersmacreative.com/social-media/employee-
engagement-via-social-media-can-improve-retention/

Brand Strategy Guru (2013 [accessed 11 October 2013]) Kickstarter is a Marketing Platform as well as a Fundraising One, *Blog: views from the world of brand and beyond* [Online] http://brandstrategyguru.com/blog/kickstarter-is-a-marketing-platform-as-well-as-a-fundraising-one

Burton, K *et al* (2013) *Best-in-class Practices in Employee Communication: Through the lens of 10 global leaders*, Institute of Public Relations, Gainesville, FL, April

Cogswell Baskin, E (2012 [accessed 11 October 2013]) Employee Engagement in a Social Media World, *Retailing Today* [Online] http://retailingtoday.com/article/employee-engagement-social-media-world

Corporate Citizenship (2013 [accessed 11 October 2013]) Future Business: The four mega-trends that every company needs to prepare for [Online] http://www.corporate-citizenship.com/our-insights/future-business-the-four-mega-trends-that-every-company-needs-to-prepare-for/

Corporate Leadership Council (2004) *Driving Performance and Retention Through Employee Engagement*, Corporate Executive Board, Washington, DC

Daye, D (2006 [accessed 11 October 2013]) History of Branding, *Branding Strategy Insider* [Online] http://www.brandingstrategyinsider.com/2006/08/history_of_bran.html#.UlgeDRCL3W8

de Chernatony, L, Drury, S and Segal-Horn, S (2004) Services brands' values: internal and external corporate communication, Open Research Online, in *Academy of Marketing Conference*, Cheltenham, UK, July

de Swaan Arons, M (2011 [accessed 11 October 2013]) How brands were born: A brief history of modern marketing, *The Atlantic* [Online] http://www.theatlantic.com/business/archive/2011/10/how-brands-were-born-a-brief-history-of-modern-marketing/246012/

Deloitte (2013 [accessed 11 October 2013]) *Human Capital Trends 2013: Leading Indicators* [Online] http://www.deloitte.com/assets/Dcom-UnitedStates/Local%20Assets/Documents/Consulting/us_cons_humancapitaltrends2013_040213.pdf

Design Council [accessed 11 October 2013] Innocent Drinks: Creative Culture and Strong Brand [Online] http://www.designcouncil.org.uk/Case-studies/Innocent-Drinks/Using-recycled-packaging-material/

EEA (2011 [accessed 11 October 2013]) Companies Lacking Employee Engagement Will Face High Turnover [Online] www.enterpriseengagement.org

Elman, A and Barry, M (2012 [accessed 11 October 2013]) The Key Lessons from the Plan A Business Case, *Marks & Spencer* [Online] http://corporate.marksandspencer.com/documents/publications/2012/plan_a_report_2012.pdf

Empathica Inc [accessed 11 October 2013] Employee Engagement [Online] http://www.empathica.com/products-services/employee-engagement/

Facebook (2012 [accessed 11 October 2013]) *Building Brands for the Connected World* [Online] https://www.facebook-studio.com/fbassets/resource/63/building_brands_whitepaper.pdf

Farquhar, R, Barrie, R, Goodwin, T *et al* (2013 [accessed 11 October 2013]) For the Love of Wispa: A Social Media-Driven Success Story, *Think Box* [Online] http://www.thinkbox.tv/server/show/ConCaseStudy.1614

Gager, S (2012 [accessed 11 October 2013]) Why Your Employer Brand Matters, *LinkedIn Talent blog* [Online] http://talent.linkedin.com/blog/index.php/2012/07/employer-brand-matters

Google+ Business [accessed 11 October 2013] Cadbury's Sweet Google+ Success, *Google+ Business* [Online] http://www.google.com/+/business/case-study/cadbury.html

Goss, F (2013 [accessed 11 October 2013]) Management Still the Biggest Barrier to Employee Engagement, *Voice, Engage for Success* [Online] http://www.engageforsuccess.org/management-still-the-biggest-barrier-to-employee-engagement/#.UaydNmRsMwE

Haigh, D (2010 [accessed 11 October 2013]) Connecting Brand Value, 'Brand Equity' and Brand Economics, *Brand Finance* [Online] http://brandfinance.com/knowledge_centre/whitepapers/connecting-brand-value-brand-equity-and-brand-economics

Havas Media Group (2013 [accessed 11 October 2013]) Meaningful Brands Factsheet, Meaningful Brands Study, *Havas Media Group* [Online] http://www.havasmedia.com/documents_library/meaningful-brands-pdfs/mb_country_factsheet_uk.pdf

Havas Media Group (2013 [accessed 11 October 2013]) Meaningful Brands, *Meaningful Brands Study* [Online] http://www.havasmedia.com/meaningful-brands

Heartbeats International (2010 [accessed 11 October 2013]) Case in Point A: Dove, Campaign for Real Beauty (4Es), *Sounds Like Branding* [Online] http://www.soundslikebranding.com/?p=1244

Herring, C (2009) Diversity in a company expands sales, profit and customer numbers, *American Sociological Review*, 74, pp 208–224

Huawei Technologies [accessed 11 October 2013] *HR Building & Culture Building in Huawei, Huawei Technologies* [Online] http://www.hruae.ae/hr-05/hcbh.pdf

Interbrand (2012 [accessed 11 October 2013]) Malaysia's Most Valuable Brands 2012, *Branding Studies* [Online] http://www.interbrand.com/en/knowledge/branding-studies.aspx

Interbrand (2013 [accessed 11 October 2013]) Best Global Brands 2012, *Interbrand* [Online] http://www.interbrand.com/en/best-global-brands/previous-years/2012/Best-Global-Brands-2012.aspx

Interbrand (2013 [accessed 11 October 2013]) Best Retail Brands 2013, *Interbrand* [Online] http://www.interbrand.com/en/ BestRetailBrands/2013/Best-Retail-Brands.aspx

JVST [accessed 11 October 2013] Intel Sponsors of Tomorrow Campaign: A Human Story for the Tech Giant, *JVST* [Online] http://www.jvst.us/ case-study/intel-sponsors-of-tomorrow-campaign/

Kapelke, C (2013 [accessed 11 October 2013]) The Big Ideal, *ANA Magazine* [Online] http://www.jimstengel.com/pdf/The_Big_Ideal.pdf

Keohane, K (2010) *The Talent Journey: The 55-minute guide to employee communications*, Verb Publishing, Royston, Herts

King, B (2012 [accessed 11 October 2013]) 50 Fastest Growing Brands Serve a 'Higher Purpose', *Sustainable Life Media* [Online] www.sustainablebrands.com

Kiss, J (2013 [accessed 11 October 2013]) Getting to grips with social media, *On Social Media Marketing*, Guardian and Media Ltd [Online] http://www.guardian.co.uk/technology/2013/jun/03/social-media-brands-jemima-kiss

Klein, M (2011) *From Lincoln to LinkedIn: The 55-minute guide to social communication*, Verb Publishing, Royston, Herts

Kurtuldu, M (2012 [accessed 11 October 2013]) Brand New: The History of Branding, *Design Today* [Online] www.designtoday.info

Lindemann, J [accessed 11 October 2013] Brand Valuation: The Financial Value of Brands, *Brand Channel* [Online] http://www.brandchannel.com/ papers_review.asp?sp_id=357

LinkedIn (2013 [accessed 11 October 2013]) LinkedIn Employer Brand Playbook: 5 Steps to Crafting a Highly Social Talent Brand, *LinkedIn* [Online] http://talent.linkedin.com/employerbrandbook/

Lucas, E (2013 [accessed 11 October 2013]) HR Hot Topics for 2013, *Ashridge Knowledge* [Online] http://www.ashridge-people.org.uk/ hr-hot-topics-for-2013/

MacLeod, D and Clarke, N (2009) *Engaging for Success: Enhancing Performance Through Employee Engagement*, Department for Business, Innovation and Skills, London

Mainwaring, S (2013) *CMO Vs. CSO: 8 Steps To Bridge The Divide That Could Undo Your Business*, CMO Network, Forbes.com

Marks & Spencer (2010 [accessed 11 October 2013]) Sustaining the Brand Promise, *Marketing Society* [Online] https://www.marketingsociety.co. uk/the-library/2010-marks-spencer-sustaining-brand-promise-case-study

Marks & Spencer (2013 [accessed 11 October 2013]) [Online] http://corporate.marksandspencer.com/

McGrory-Dixon, A (2013 [accessed 11 October 2013]) Social Media: A Tool to Boost Employee Engagement, Productivity, *Benefitspro* [Online] http://www.benefitspro.com/2013/04/19/social-media-a-tool-to-boost-employee-engagement-p

Melcrum [accessed 11 October 2013] Inside Internal Communication: Groundbreaking Innovations for a New Future, *Meldrum* [Online] https://www.melcrum.com/internal-communication

Meyer, R (2013 [accessed 11 October 2013]) A History of Green Brands 1960s and 1970s – Doing the Groundwork, *Fast Company, Mansueto Ventures* [Online] http://www.fastcompany.com/1568686/history-green-brands-1960s-and-1970s—doing-groundwork

Millward Brown Optimor and WPP (2013 [accessed 11 October 2013]) *BrandZ™ Top 100 Most Valuable Global Brands 2013* [Online] http://www.millwardbrown.com/brandz/2013/Top100/Docs/2013_BrandZ_Top100_Report.pdf

Moreland, J (2013 [accessed 11 October 2013]) The Costs of Ignoring Employee Engagement, *Fast Company* [Online] http://www.fastcompany.com/3009012/the-costs-of-ignoring-employee-engagement

O'Brien, J (2012 [accessed 11 October 2013]) Four Steps for Recognising Employees in a Virtual Workplace, *Bi Worldwide* [Online] http://www.biworldwide.co.uk/white-papers/detail/four-steps-for-recognising-employees-in-a-virtual-workplace

Olins, W (2002 [accessed 11 October 2013]) Corporate Identity – The Ultimate Resource, *Viewpoints* [Online] http://www.wallyolins.com/views.htm

Paladino, J (2010 [accessed 11 October 2013]) How IBM Promotes Employee Engagement with Social Media, *Write Speak Sell* [Online] http://writespeaksell.com/how-ibm-promotes-employee-engagement-with-social-media

Petrook, M (2009 [accessed 11 October 2013]) Half of Workers Quit Jobs due to Bad Management, *Chartered Management Institute* [Online] http://www.managers.org.uk/news/half-workers-quit-jobs-due-bad-management

PwC (2013) *The Talent Challenge: A Time for Extraordinary Leadership*, 16th Annual Global CEO Survey, PwC, London

Quek, C (2013 [accessed 11 October 2013]) Make Your Brand Story Meaningful, *Harvard Business Review Blogs* [Online] http://blogs.hbr.org/2013/06/make-your-brand-story-meaningf/

Richardson, N D (2012 [accessed 11 October 2013]) A Quick History of Branding, *The Branding Spot* [Online] http://ndrichardson.com/blog/2012/07/03/a-quick-history-of-branding/

Roth, B (2013 [accessed 11 October 2013]) Green Sells: Meaningful Brands Outperform the Stock Market, *Triple Pundit* [Online] http://www.triplepundit.com/2013/06/green-sells-meaningful-brands-outperform-stock-market/

Ruck, K [accessed 11 October 2013] Exploring Internal Engagement: Towards Informed Employee Voice [Online] http://www.exploringinternalcommunication.com/authors/

Rutgers Media (2009 [accessed 11 October 2013]) History of branding... The battle for Your Dollar, *Rutgers Media* [Online] http://www.youtube.com/watch?v=X5rx4m2DL-A

Sascha (2012 [accessed 11 October 2013]) Social Media as a Brand Building Tool, *Wire GmbH* [Online] http://www.wearewire.com/social-media-as-a-brand-building-tool/

Schept, K (2013 [accessed 11 October 2013]) BrandZTM Top 100 Most Valuable Global Brands 2013, *Millward Brown and WPP* [Online] http://www.millwardbrown.com/brandz/2013/Top100/Docs/2013_BrandZ_Top100_Report.pdf

Schwartz, A (2013 [accessed 11 October 2013]) Businesses with a Strong Sense of Purpose Are More Successful, *Co.EXIST, Fast Company* [Online] http://www.fastcoexist.com/1682123/businesses-with-a-strong-sense-of-purpose-are-more-successful

Silverman, M, Bakhshalian, E and Hillman, L (2013) *Social Media and Employee Voice: The current landscape*, Chartered Institute of Personnel and Development, London

Silverstein, B (2013 [accessed 11 October 2013]) Coca-Cola Gets Personal in Europe with 'Share a Coke' Campaign, *Brand Channel* [Online] http://www.brandchannel.com/home/post/Coke-Share-Campaign-051513.aspx

Simpson, K [accessed 11 October 2013] Top 10 Branding Examples Killing It and What You Can Learn From Them, *Big Girl Branding* [Online] http://www.biggirlbranding.com/top-10-branding-examples-killing-it-and-what-you-can-learn-from-them/

Stokes, T (2013) *Want To Know Your Secret Brand Building Weapon? Sshh, It's Your Employees*, Forrester Research

Stokes, T M, Cooperstein, D, Munchbach, C and Dernoga, M (2012) *How Social Media is Changing Brand Building*, Forrester Research

Stratmann, J (2012 [accessed 11 October 2013]) Using Social Media to Improve Communications [Online] http://www.simply-communicate.com/case-studies/case-study/using-social-media-improve-internal-communications

Tesseras, L (2013 [accessed 11 October 2013]) The Best of British Brand Performers, *Marketing Week* [Online] http://www.marketingweek.co.uk/trends/the-best-of-british-brand-performers/4006338.article

The Corporate Executive Board Company (2012) *Global Workforce Insights Quarterly Report*, Author, Arlington, VA

The Times 100 & Wilson and Wilson Publishing Ltd [accessed 11 October 2013] Building an airline through brand values: A Virgin Atlantic case study, *The Times 100 Business Case Studies* [Online] http://businesscasestudies.co.uk/virgin-atlantic/building-an-airline-through-brand-values/the-branson-factor.html#ixzz2UgmTnzpJ

The Times 100 and Wilson and Wilson Publishing Ltd [accessed 11 October 2013] *SWOT Analysis and Sustainable Business Planning: An IKEA Case Study* [Online] http://businesscasestudies.co.uk/ikea/ swot-analysis-and-sustainable-business-planning/conclusion. html#axzz2ZrfuW4hw

Times Newspapers Ltd (2012 [accessed 11 October 2013]) The Sunday Times Best 100 Companies, *The Sunday Times* [Online] http://features. thesundaytimes.co.uk/public/best100companies

Towers Watson (2013 [accessed 11 October 2013]) 2013 Towers Watson Change and Communication ROI Survey [Online] http://www.towerswatson.com/en/Press/2013/05/just-over-half-of- employers-using-social-media-tools-for-internal-communication

Wadee, Z (2013 [accessed 11 October 2013]) Facebook Your Boss: Using Social Media in Internal Communications, *Guardian Careers* [Online] Guardian News and Media Ltd, http://careers.guardian.co.uk/ careers-blog/facebook-employers-encourage-social-media

Wood, L (2000) Brands and brand equity: definition and management, *Management Decision*, 38 (9), pp 662–69

Yammer [accessed 11 October 2013] [Online] https://www.yammer.com/ solutions/employee-engagement/

Zybowski, A (2013 [accessed 11 October 2013]) BrandZ™ Top 100 Most Valuable Global Brands 2013, *BrandZ and Millward Brown* [Online] http://www.millwardbrown.com/brandz/2013/Top100/Docs/2013_ BrandZ_Top100_Report.pdf

INDEX

NB: page numbers in *italic* indicate figures or tables

Advertising Research Foundation   124
Allen, D   16
Amazon   106
ambition   113–16, 117, 121 *see also*
        definitions *and* strategy
    of different organizations   114–15
    and purposes   113–14 *see also* P-A-S-P
        model
Amuso, L   96–97
Anderson, R   108
Apple   25, 33
    and packaging design   38
articles (on)
    diversity (*Harvard Business Review*)   78
    Sears and employee engagement (*Harvard
        Business Review*)   54
authentic, relevant and differentiating   67

Beer, M   115–16
Benson, B
a better way   *see* change
blog on lists and rule of three (Listly)   81–82
Brand Asset Valuator (Young & Rubicam)
    15
brand definition (and)   20–32
    the challenge   26
    challenges with the current state   27–29
    current state of practice   20–26
        see brand definition methods
    the problem   29–32 *see also* Huawei
    website for   25
brand definition methods   20–26
    definition: brand models   23–26
        see also brand models
    discovery   21–23
        position   22–23
brand delivery (and)   33–42
    customer and user experience   36, 36, 37
    customer brand engagement   40
    employee brand engagement   41–42
    guidelines for   35–36
    method(s) for   34–35
    touch points for   34
    user experience mapping   37–40, 39
        brand advocacy   38–39
        brand awareness   37

brand consideration   37–38
brand departure   39–40, 39
brand experience   38
brand selection (preference)   38
    objective   33–34
brand and diversity (and)   161–67
        see also Brooke, B *and* diversity
    diversity and inclusiveness   161–62
    experience of inclusivity and diversity
        164–65
    feel of the marketplace   165
    functional diversity   164
    gender perspectives   164
    inclusive leadership   163–64
    qualifying for leadership   166
    research on diverse teams   162–63
    ways to demonstrate diversity and
        inclusivity   165
    what matters from a brand perspective
        167
    women as economically high-growth
        market   166
brand equity (Moran): effective market
        share; relative price; durability   15
brand and executive talent (and)   157–60
    bottom line for senior-level hires   160
    categories of can-do, will-do and fit   158
    the culture fit   158–59
    culture variation and senior talent   159
    diversity   160
    driving a different culture   159
    recruiting at senior level   157
brand models   23–26
    brand architecture   25–26
    brand attributes   23–24
        Huawei example of   24
    brand essence/DNA   23
    brand promise   25
    brand values   25
brand in a multinational conglomerate
        183–89 *see* Mahindra Group *and*
        Shukla, S P
brand positioning: authentic, different and
        relevant   18
brand and purpose   190–96 *see also*
        Johnson & Johnson *and* Sneed, M

brand and social media   43–50 *see also*
   social media
brand and talent   197–201 *see also* EY
   (Ernst & Young) *and* Weinberger, M
brand, talent and the new world of work
   (and)   168–74 *see also* Coplin, D
   and Microsoft
   agility   172
   evolution of branding industry and
      emergence of social media   170
   organizations oriented around common
      goals   171–72
   outmoded models and ways of thinking
      169–70
   solutions   172–73
brand, talent and strategy (and)   175–82
   see also Cullen, M *and* Ernst &
   Young (EY)
   business linkage study   177–78
   effect of skills shortage   176–77
   engagement drivers   179–80
   from financial services to global
      people leader   175–76
   HR   181–82
   new EVP and brand positioning for EY
      176
   new purpose of EY   180–81
   people engagement   180
brand valuation (and)   15–16
   assessing attributes (Aker and others)   15
   brand equity (Moran)   15
      see also subject entry
   concept and London Stock Exchange   15
   methods   15–16
branding, history of   8–9, 10
brand(s)   7–19
   brief history of   7, 8–10
   as business management discipline
      16–17
   concluding questions on   19
   examples of great   10, 11–12
   marketing and sales   13–14, 13, 14
   positioning as authentic, relevant and
      different   18
   premium   17–18
   and setting the context   7
   talent   1–2
   valuation *see* brand valuation
BrandPic   2, 87
The BrandZ Top 100 Most Valuable Brands
   (Interbrand annual report)   15
Brooke, B   79, 161–67
   background to role at EY   161–62
Business Reimagined   92
business-as-usual (BAU   80

CapGemini Applications   2
change   91–103
   begins (by/with)
      auditing your competition   101
      auditing yourself   99, 100–101
      banning specific words/phrases   92–93
      committing and executing   102
      a core framework   95–99, 96, 98, 99
         see also P-A-S-P model
      designing possible solutions and
         engaging people again   101–02
      engaging stakeholders   100, 101
      keeping one brand and one core set of
         ideas   93–99, 94
      values   96–97
   communications   73–74
   difference of approach to   102–03
   and making the connection   91–92
chapter notes/references for
   ambition   116
   brand and social media   50
   brand delivery   42
   brand(s)   19
   change   103
   defining your brand   32
   engaging talent   87
   proposition   128
   purpose   112
   putting it all together   140
   strategy   122
   the talent agenda   62
   toolkit   153
chapter summaries/conclusions (for)
   ambition   116
   brand and social media   50
   brands   19
   engaging talent   86
   purpose   111–12
   putting it all together   139
   strategy   121–22
Churchill, W   81, 82
Coca-Cola   70, 107
codes of conduct   70
Collins, J   96
communication(s)
   change   73–74
   employee   75–76
   two-way   75
consumer marketing approaches   27
Coplin, D   61, 92, 168–74
   as chief envisioning officer at Microsoft
      UK   168–69
Corporate Identity   34
'The Corporate Personality: an inquiry into the
   nature of corporate identity'   34

corporate purpose, ambition, strategy and
        positioning   132
crises, surviving major   40
Cullen, M   175–82

defining your brand   *see* brand definition
definitions (of)
    ambition   113
    customer value proposition   127
    diversity   77
    employment value proposition   127
    purpose   105
    social communication   45
    strategy   117
The Discipline of Market Leaders   17
Disney   107
    purpose and ambition   115
diversity   77–79, 160
    brand   *see* brand and diversity
    functional   164
    HBR article on   78
    and inclusivity   164–65
    and performance studies   77–78

Edelman's Trust Barometer   45
Einstein, A   79
employee communication   75–76
employee lifecycle (and)   64–75, 65
    joining experience   69–70
    recruitment experience   68–69
    risks of 'employee branding' efforts
        67–68
    your brand   65–66
    your talent brand   66–58
    work experience (in)   70–75
        change communications   73–74
        departure experience   74–75
        employee brand engagement   72–73
        talent management/career
            development   71–72
employment value proposition (EVP)
        67–70, 72–74, 176, 179
engagement, top five drivers of   80
engaging talent (and)   63–87
    diversity   77–79 *see also subject entry*
    employee communications: the three
        Ms   75
    employee lifecycle   64–75, 65
        see also subject entry
    fundamental points for   75–76
    information overload/fatigue syndrome
        79–80
    as a journey   63–64
    measurement   83–86 *see also subject entry*
    media   83

messages   79–82, 81
    'religion, repetition, trios' example
        of   81–82
    more integrated approach to   86–87
    situational leadership   76
EY (Ernst & Young)   2, 79, 106, 114,
        175–82, 197–201 *see also* brand
        and talent; Brooke, B; Cullen, M
        and Weinberger, M
    Global Talent Function   175
    importance of purpose   199
    purpose and ambition   115, 121
    and Vision 2020   200

Facebook   40, 83
figures
    blank messaging framework   *152*
    the brand marketing funnel   *13*
    a brand positioning spectrum   *125, 144*
    the Corporate Executive Board
        Company's model   *56*
    the Corporate Leadership Council's model
        of engagement   *55*
    efficient vs inefficient conversion   *14*
    the employee lifecycle   *65*
    how P-A-S-P drives Awareness,
        Consideration, Preference and
        Advocacy   *126*
    master P-A-S-P model   *153*
    a messaging framework   *81*
    P-A-S-P model   *105, 135*
    P-A-S-P model examples   *136*
    purpose, ambition, strategy,
        proposition   *145*
    stakeholder mapping – the broader
        community   *148*
    stakeholder mapping – competitors   *150*
    stakeholder mapping – customers/clients
        149
    stakeholder mapping – stakeholders   *151*
    stakeholder mapping – third-party
        organizations   *147*
    stakeholder mapping – your
        organization   *146*
    value disciplines   *142*
    variations on the 'customer lifecycle
        marketing' theme   *37*
    why do people leave brands?   *39*
Forbes on brands   110
Ford, H   xv, 31
Fred Reichheld, Bain & Company   16

gender diversity   78, 183
Giblin, E   96–97
globalization   74, 95, 187–88

Harvard Business Review   54, 78, 109
    see also articles
Harvard Business School   77, 115
Havas Global   110
Hay Group   31
Heskett, J   54
Huawei   29–31, 41–42, 64, 80, 91
    brand attributes   24, 25
    core values   29
    definition of culture of   29–30
Hubbard, D W   83

IBM (and)   25, 31, 106, 108, 114
    key areas for creating a 'smarter planet'
        119–20
    'Solutions for a smarter planet'   118
    strategy   118–20
Incorporated Society of British Advertisers
    (ISBA)   133
insight interviews   *see subject entries*
        and named persons as detailed in
        contents pages
Interface   94, 108

Johnson, R W   190
Johnson & Johnson (and)   82, 190–96
        see also Sneed, M
    air traffic control/noise
        management   193–95
    barriers and challenges   191
    credo of   190, 192, 194
    engaging people and candidates in credo
        and values   192–93
    level of engagement   193
    risks of top-down approach   195–96
Jones, D   110

KitKat®   26
Klein, M   45

Lace, J   133
leadership
    inclusive   163–64
    qualifying for   166
    situational   76
lists: rule of three examples – religion,
        repetition, trios   81–82

McKinsey & Company   106
    purpose and ambition   115
Mahindra Group (and)   183–89
    concept of A1 companies   184
    connecting brand and talent: group
        management centre (GMC)   185–86
    core ideas and purpose   186–87
    globalization   187–88

House of Mahindra   186–87
    HR   189
    manufacturing background of   188
    new word mark   188–89
    recruitment from humanities
        background   188
    Rise tag line   189
    Visual Identity   183
measurement, messages and media
        (the three Ms)   75
measurement   83–86
    qualitative approaches to   86
    quantitative approaches to   84–85
    and risks   84–85
Microsoft   61, 92, 168–73
Millward Brown   110
mission   64, 102
MIT Sloan School of Management   77
models
    CLC engagement   55–56, 55
    PAP   117
    P-A-S-P   *see* P-A-S-P model
    situational leadership   76

National Organizations Survey   78
Nestle®   26
net promoter score (NPS)   16

Ogilvy, D   7
Olins, W   34
One Young World   110

Palmisano, S   108
P-A-S-P model   95–99, 96, 98, 99, 104–05,
        105, 114, 118, 123, 126, 129,
        134–35, 135, 136–38, 139, 144,
        145, 152–53, 153
Peters, T   96
Polman, P   108, 121
Porras, J   96
Porter, M   118, 129
positioning   102, 123–26, 125
    infrastructure-led   124
    process-led   125
    product or service-led   124–25
    purpose-led   126, 126
    values-led   125–26
PriceWaterhouseCoopers (PwC)   31
Procter & Gamble (P&G)   26, 27, 40, 107,
        108
proposition (and)   123–28 *see also*
        definitions; P-A-S-P model *and*
        positioning
    customer value   127
    the deal   123
    employment value   127–28

Psychology Today   124
purpose (and)   104–12
    as brand model   106
    defining   105
    four-box (P-A-S-P) model   104–05, *105*
        see also P-A-S-P model
    purpose-driven brands   106–11
        see also subject entry
purpose-driven brands   106–11
    do better, evidence for   109–11
    examples of   106–07
    and J&J's credo   107–08
    leaders' comments on   108–09
    three simple rules for   110–11
putting it all together (and)   129–40
        see also P-A-S-P model
    employer branding   131, 132
    friction points   130
    the integrated approach   133–34
        see also surveys
    network analysis   134–55, *135*, *136*
    other functions   137, *137–38*
    putting P-A-S-P to work   129
    reputation as brand   131–33
    testing the approach   139

Quinn, S (Walmart CMO)   45

Reichheld, F   54
research (on)
    diverse teams   162–63
    drivers of engagement (CLC)   80
    emotions and brands (*Psychology Today*)
        124
    employee engagement (Gallup)   54–55
    link between talent programs and
        improved return on business capital/
        performance 177
    social media (Forrester)   43, 44
    top five drivers of engagement (CLC)   80
rule of three: religion, repetition, trios   81–82

SAP   106, 109
    purpose and ambition   114
Sasser, W E Jr   54
Satmetrix   16
Shukla, S P   183–89 *see also* Mahindra
        Group
situational leadership   76
slogans   106–07
Smith, A   53
Snabe, J H   109
Sneed, M   82, 190–96 *see also* Johnson &
        Johnson
social media (as)   43–50, 170 *see also*
    definitions

external brand engagement tool   49–50
Facebook white paper on   44–45
Forrester research report on   43, 44
internal tool   45, 49, *46–48*
social communication – technologically
        enabled   45
Stanford Graduate School of Business
        Diversity and Work Group
        Performance faculty   77
Stengel, J   108, 110
strategy   64, 117–22
    examples   118–21, *121 see also* EY; IBM
        and Unilever
    plan   117–18
Stuart, J   14
studies (of/on)
    Brand Finance and Global 500   15
    emotions towards brands   124
    global analytical framework on brands
        (Havas Media Group)   109–10
        check this
    information fatigue syndrome (IFS)
        (Reuter)   79–80
    market leaders   17
    social media (Insight Consulting)   43–44
    talent diversity and brand (US)   78
    values (Giblin and Amuso)   96–97
summaries   *see* chapter summaries
surveys (by/on)
    46 global marketers on integration
        (FlockAssociates)   133–34
    global CEO survey (PWC)   56
    market's view on integration
        (ISBA/Professor J Lace)   133

tables
    brief history of branding   *8–9*
    customer and user experience:
        things to consider   36
    examples of alignment to P-A-S-P   *137–38*
    examples of great brands   *11–12*, *12*
    functional ownership of brands   *59–60*
    snapshot of social media for brand
        building   *46–48*
    Unilever's 'Sustainable Living Plan'   *121*
the talent agenda (and)   53–62
    CLC engagement model   55–56, *55*
    CLC's HR EVP framework   56–57, *56*
    employee engagement   53–55, 61
        history of   54–55
    functional ownership of brand and talent
        agenda   58, 60–62, *59–60*
    reasons why organizations struggle   57–58
*The Talent Journey: The 55-minute guide to
        employee communications*   3
Taylor, F W   xv, 31

toolkit exercises   141–53
    1: value disciplines   141–43, *142*
      a. product/service leadership   142–43
      b. operational excellence   143
      c. customer/marketplace intimacy   143
    2: positioning   *144*, 144
    3: purpose, ambition, strategy, positioning
      145, *145*
    4: stakeholders   145, *146*, *147*, *148*,
      149, *150*, *151*
    5: messaging framework   *152*, 152
    6: bringing it all together   152–53, *153*
Treacy, M   17
Twitter   40

Unilever   26, 27, 106, 107
    purpose and ambition of   114
    sustainable living plan   120–21, *121*

values   64, 102
Virgin   26
vision   64, 102

Walmart   45
war for talent   56
Waterman, B   96
Weinberger, M (and)   108–09, 197–201
    see also EY (Ernst & Young)
    challenges faced as CEO   198
    exceptional experience at EY   199
    insights as Chairman and CEO   201
    inspirational purpose   200
    interaction of brand management and
      talent management   201
Welch, J   160
Wharton Business School (University of
    Pennsylvania)   77
what is a brand?   *see* brand(s)
'Why Your Employer Brand Matters'
    (LinkedIn White Paper, 2012)   66
Wiersema, F   17
workforces, Gallup data on benefits of highly
    engaged   54–55

Zuckerberg, M   83